COMPUTER

PROGRAMMING
FOR
EVERYONE

KEITH LEE

Programming for *Everyone*

ISBN: 978-1-105-56855-8

More information about this book, as well as access to other related resources, is available at **www.motupresse.com**.

To the Three Amigos

Contents

About the Author

Keith Lee is a Software Architect and Engineer who has been implementing software systems for over 20 years. He has a vast range of experience implementing desktop applications, distributed (server-side) systems, and software for mobile devices. He is the author of several books and articles on technology, most recently the book **Core Objective-C** *in 24 Hours*.

Preface

We use computers everyday; they have become an essential part of our lives. Perhaps as you read this you have a computer in your possession (for example a cell phone or device), are about to use a computer-controlled machine (maybe a car or a tool), or just have a computer in operation nearby (in your house, at the bookstore, really just about anywhere). So, we are very comfortable with computers and the computer programs that actually make them useful, but have you ever wondered how all this stuff works? Well, **Programming for *Everyone*** answers these questions. It is designed to provide you with a basic understanding of programming, maybe even inspiring you to take the next step and begin developing your own programs. The book is geared towards a very general audience, and prior programming experience is not required. Enough said; now are you ready and set? Great, then let's get started!

Chapter 1
Introduction

The title says it all; **Programming for *Everyone*** is designed to give
the reader a general introduction to computer programming. And it's
not just for people who are already comfortable with computer-
speak; the book is written for a very general audience and focuses
on providing you with a detailed understanding of the basic concepts.
It's also great for those of you who want to look into other areas of
programming (e.g. logic programming, computer graphics, games,
etc.) that you may not have experience in. Plenty of references are
provided if you want to find out more about any of the topics covered
in this book. Hopefully after reading this you'll do just that!

About This Book

The ultimate goal of this book is to help people gain a better
understanding of the technology that's so pervasive in our daily lives.
At first, to those not involved in the Information Technology (IT) field,
computer programming can seem extremely complex and even
somewhat intimidating. The book aims to eliminate that impression
by explaining programming concepts in a way that's clear and
understandable, while also providing examples that aid
comprehension. You're free to read the book cover-to-cover, or go
directly to specific chapters of interest. Either way, you'll find plenty
of information to give you a good start in the world of computer
programming.

Typographical Conventions

The following typographical conventions are used in this book:

Bold font style within the body of text indicates significant words or phrases. Bold is also used to identify chapters or sections within a chapter.

Italics font style indicates new words or phrases that are explained further in the body of the book.

`Monospaced, constant width` font is used for programming code excerpts and examples.

`Monospaced, constant width bold` font is used within programming code excerpts and examples to indicate key elements and concepts.

`Monospaced, constant width italic` font is used within programming code excerpts to indicate comments.

How to use This Book

This book is organized in a way that combines programming theory with application. Specifically the chapters on general programming concepts and principles alternate with those that explore a particular programming language or topic and include practical examples. This organization is designed to make it easy to read the book straight through or by picking and choosing chapters according to the topics that interest you most. With that in mind here's a brief overview of the book's contents.

Chapter 2: *Qu'est-ce que c'est?*
(What is this?) This chapter is designed to introduce the reader to computer programming by providing a brief overview of programming languages and the different programs we write with them.

Chapter 3: *Parlez-vous Objective-C?*
Here you will learn about object-oriented programming and begin studying your first programming language, Objective-C.

Chapter 4: *Language Types*
In this chapter we'll look at the different types of programming languages there are, how they are used, and how you might go about selecting a language for writing a program.

Chapter 5: *Welcome to My World (Wide Web)*
Here you actually begin writing programs! We'll start with an overview of HTML, the foundation for web programming. Then you get to create your first web page using HTML, CSS, and JavaScript.

Chapter 6: *Dissecting the Machine*
Maybe it's not actually necessary to understand the internals of a computer in order to write programs, but we're going to learn about

this anyway. In this chapter we'll look at the key components of a computer and learn exactly how it's used to execute programs.

Chapter 7: *Social Networking*
Social networking websites continue to grow and acquire more users; in fact it seems like just about everyone who uses a computer these days has an account on one or more of these websites. Here we look at social networking platforms and how they work, and then you get to apply this knowledge by writing your first Facebook app.

Chapter 8: *The Programmer's Toolkit*
Having the right tools, and knowing how to use them, can make your computer programming experience both more efficient and more enjoyable. This chapter introduces the principle tools and utilities you'll use for writing programs, along with tips on their usage.

Chapter 9: *Going Mobile*
Many of you reading this book have one or more mobile devices and use mobile apps almost daily. In this chapter you'll learn about programming for mobile devices and write some code for a mobile app.

Chapter 10: *Secure Coding*
We hear stories all the time about websites being hacked and valuable information stored on computers being stolen. This chapter is all about writing secure programs; it starts by identifying common computer security threats, and then presents recommendations for developing secure programs.

Chapter 11: *Computer Graphics*
There are numerous programming languages and tools for creating digital images and animations. This chapter provides an introduction to computer graphics and its main specialties, provides an overview of several representative graphics languages and libraries, and concludes with a couple of hands-on examples where you learn how to create computer animations and 3D graphics.

Chapter 12: *Game Programming*
Game programming can be almost as much fun as actually playing games themselves. In this chapter you'll learn the basics of game programming, and then look at some code for a simple game.

Chapter 13: *Next Steps*
This chapter provides a recap of the topics and material covered in this book, along with some additional pointers for learning more about computer programming.

Appendix A: Prolog
Logic programming is a particular style of programming that implements relations and employs mathematical logic to specify

solutions to problems. This Appendix presents an overview of logic programming and **Prolog**, the most commonly used logic programming language.

Appendix B: Glossary
The glossary includes definitions for many of the key concepts and terms used in this book.

Appendix C: References
This Appendix lists useful references that are valuable to the reader looking for more information on the subjects covered in this book.

Attention New Programmers!
Particularly for beginners, computer programming can be a little frustrating at first. Here are a few recommendations that will be very helpful when you start writing programs:

- **<u>Proper syntax</u>** - It is **very** important that your program code has the correct syntax. Specifically, capitalization, spacing, and other syntax elements should be identical to that shown in this book and the reference documentation. In general computers and programming languages are very strict about syntax, so if you make typing errors your program will not run properly.
- **<u>Check your work</u>** – Mistakes happen, so check your work frequently, particularly just before you run your programs.
- **<u>One step at a time</u>** – Develop your programs incrementally. This means write small portions of code, test and fix errors until you verify the code works as expected, and add more code to your program accordingly.

Questions and Comments
There's a lot of material here to digest, so go slowly and don't press; it will sink in over time. With this approach I'm confident that you'll become more confident and capable using computers and computer programs.

If at any time you have questions about this book or would like to leave a comment or suggestion, please stop by the website http://www.motupresse.com/p4e. Your feedback is greatly appreciated!

Chapter 2
Qu'est-ce que c'est?
(What is this?)

Let's assume that you have no programming experience at all, but have used computers (by now, that's just about everyone). So, why do you want to learn about programming? Are you being forced to because of a class you're enrolled in, are you having problems communicating with a geek, are you looking to impress a friend, or do just want to try something completely different? Whatever your reason, we'll start off with a basic explanation of computer programming and discuss some of the ways that programs are used.

You can find multiple definitions for the word ***program,*** the one we'll use here is this

- *A program is a planned sequence of events or structured activities.*

A person who writes programs is working as a *programmer*, and *computer programming* is the action of writing a program(s) to be executed on a computer.

Now that we know what computer programming is, the next question is, why do it? Well I'm not going to get into an explanation of computers and what they're good for, but let's just say that a computer is a machine that can be used to carry out instructions that perform computations, control a device, process information, etc. – the list is only limited by our imaginations.

Simply know this boys and girls, *computers and computer programs make the world a better place*! So, this is how it goes – you write a computer program that has the instructions you want performed, load the program on a computer, tell the computer to execute the program, and that's pretty much it. Sounds pretty simple, eh? It really is that simple, at least conceptually. Let's say that you want to write a program to display on your computer screen a welcome message and the current time, like this

Hello, World!
The current time is 2012-02-10 07:50:58 PST

You know what you want the computer to do, so you just put those instructions in the program and that's it, right? But wait a minute, how do you write it so that the computer will do what you want it to do? I mean, how do you write a program so that the computer will understand and carry out your instructions? This is where *computer-programming languages* become important.

Programming Languages - An Overview

Programming languages have been around for a long time. Some of the earliest were used for things like player pianos and textile machines (specifically, piano roles are programs for player pianos). A computer programming language is used to create instructions for the activities you want a computer to perform. So if a programming language was based on a *natural* language (say English), the simple program we mentioned above might have the following instructions:

- Display the message "Hello, World!"
- Display the current date and time.

If a computer could execute these instructions *"as-is"* – in other words it understood English – you could just create a new file, type in these instructions, and tell the computer to *process* the file (i.e. execute the program). On your monitor you would then see the welcome message followed by the current date and time! Unfortunately, computer programs (at least the vast majority in use today and the ones we'll discuss here) are not written in natural languages; they are written in *artificial* programming languages. This is because computers don't understand English, they understand the language of computers, which is to say they live in the land of bits, bytes, registers, instruction sets, and numerous other things incomprehensible to people who don't inhabit the world of Geek. So, in order to write a computer program you have to learn a new language!

Language Components

As mentioned above, programming languages are used to communicate instructions to a machine, in this case a computer. Fundamentally these instructions typically do two things: 1) describe or define data (structures), and 2) perform operations on data (like arithmetic, comparisons, transformations, etc.). The instructions must follow a specific form, or *syntax*, so that the computer can execute them properly.

In order to use a programming language you need to understand its *syntax* (what it looks like) and its *semantics* (what it means). Now a programming language's syntax can be thought of as its *grammar* – the rules that define the combination of symbols for a correctly structured program. Just as with a natural language you have to use words from an accepted vocabulary, construct your sentences and paragraphs properly, etc., there are corresponding rules for writing programs. Semantics for most programming languages refers to how a computer processes a syntactically correct, complete grammatical element in the language (for example, it executes an instruction, accesses data, etc.).

Basic Elements

The basic elements for most programming languages are *symbols, numbers,* and *expressions*. A programming language **symbol** is somewhat like a word in a natural language – an element of content with practical meaning. In most programming languages symbols are commonly written as a letter followed by zero or more of any characters (excluding whitespace). There are many uses for symbols in programming languages; for example a *variable* holds a value and is named with a symbol. Many programming languages also support a set of **operators**: an operator is a symbol(s) that performs an instruction like addition (+) or subtraction (-). A **number** is an unbroken sequence of one or more decimal digits, optionally preceded by a plus or minus sign. An **expression** is a group of one or more numbers and/or symbols that can be evaluated and return a value. An expression is somewhat like a phrase in a natural language. There are many types of expressions: mathematical expressions, comparison expressions, etc. For example, a mathematical expression to add two numbers might be something like this

```
10 + 20
```

Many programming languages support the notion of *statements*. A programming **statement** can be considered as a complete, standalone language element, somewhat like a sentence in a natural language. It is comprised of symbols, numbers, and/or expressions and is commonly terminated by a symbol or a newline (the specific statement terminator used is programming language-dependent). Each statement within a computer program maps to data and one or more machine instructions. Statements are used for many purposes: assigning a value to a variable, controlling the flow of execution of instructions, executing grouped sections of program *code*, etc. The previous example can be modified to add two numbers and assign the sum to a variable named `result` with the following code

```
result = 10 + 20;
```

This example is an *assignment statement;* assignment statements typically assign a value to a variable. Notice that a semicolon is used to terminate the statement. Most programming languages also support *functions* (also known as subroutines, procedures, routines, methods, or subprograms). A **function** is a portion of code within a program that performs a specific task and is relatively independent of the remaining program code. Functions enable you to break a program down into small, well-defined units of code. Functions can be executed one or many times within a program, be executed at any time and from within many places in a program (including from other functions), and can take values for input and return a value(s) as a result of execution. Let's say, for example, that you need to perform a certain set of operations multiple times within a program. Instead of writing these instructions multiple times within the program, you write a function containing them and execute it each time the set of operations must be performed. Functions are usually named with a symbol and can also be executed within the context of an expression.

Program Components
Now that we understand these basic elements of a program, what do we do with them? We know that a program includes the elements specified above, but how are they turned into an

executable program? In order to answer this question it makes sense to look at the components of a computer program and how they work together. These common components are the program executable, software libraries, and program data.

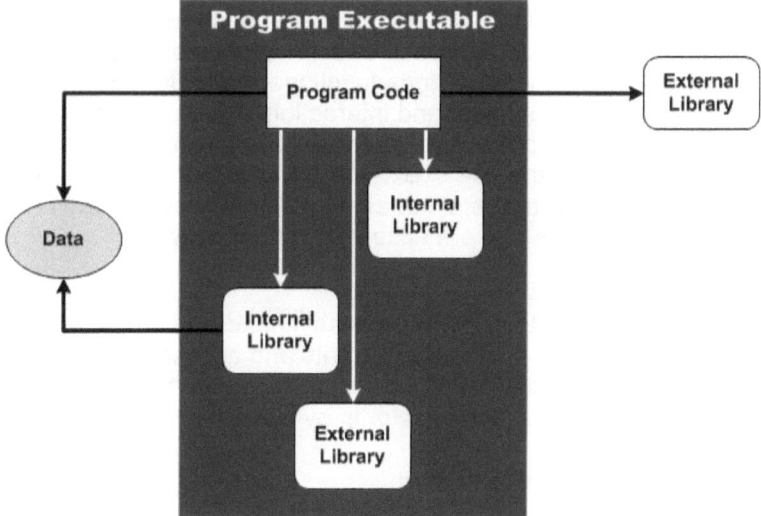

Figure 1. Basic Program Components

Executable

Within the context of computer programming, an executable file consists of the program code executed by the computer. The code may be translated into instructions that can be directly executed by the computer, or it may be in some other form (if executed by an interpreter for example). An executable may include/access multiple files; some may be program code specifically written by the programmer and some may be reusable code packaged in one or more software libraries. In such cases the programming language may include a tool (a *linker*) that combines these files into a single executable program. Linking may be performed statically, i.e. before program execution begins, or dynamically (during program execution).

Software Library

In computer programming a library is a collection of resources used to develop software. Libraries enable the reuse of code and data that provides common services; a library may consist of resources such as

- Functions/subroutines
- Class object definitions
- Globally available values and variables
- Standard resources (common data files, etc.)

Many programming languages include one or more standard libraries that are made available for every implementation of the language. They typically include functionality for standard algorithms, data structures, and interaction with the computer system (e.g. data input/output, operating system services, etc.). Many also support the use of external libraries during program execution; at the extreme external libraries may even reside on separate computers and are accessed over a network.

Data
Programs use data to perform processing and transmit results. This data may be in a variety of formats and accessed by any supported data sources. Program input/output (I/O) with external data sources is a significant factor in overall program execution.

Simplifying With Abstractions
Programming languages are designed to be clear and concise. Fundamentally, computer programs are all about manipulating data and executing instructions. However, the details of the computer hardware and the actual instructions it can execute are very machine-specific; they don't map well to the actual problems we are trying to solve. Now let's suppose that a programming language includes features that allow us to more closely represent the actual problem solution we want to implement (like implementing an algorithm, sorting data, etc.). In this case, we can greatly improve our efficiency at writing programs; in fact, programming languages do just this with *abstractions*. Now this might seem a little counterintuitive at first; in fact you may be thinking, when something is abstract isn't it less clear? Well it really depends upon your perspective. In the field of computer programming, abstractions allow us to focus on the details relevant to the problem at hand, and not the specifics of the computer hardware on which to implement (in a program) the problem solution. For example, let's say we need to create a program that performs the computation *180 ÷ pi* (where *pi* = 3.14159), and stores the result in a variable named `radiansToDegrees`. Now we want to implement this program with a programming language that directly reflects that equation, and doesn't require us to translate it into computer terms that

hide its meaning. In other words, we would like to use a programming language to write code like this for the above equation

```
radiansToDegrees = 180.0 / 3.14159;
```

This code is easy to understand and also directly corresponds to the equation. Pretty simple so far, but let's say we want to perform a certain computation multiple times during the course of program execution, or want to use a variable to represent a value (like `radiansToDegrees` above), how do we do that? This is the value of abstractions; most programming languages contain abstractions for data and instructions; they provide mechanisms used for organizing data and also controlling how a program's instructions are executed.

If a programming language has no abstractions it is *machine code,* and executes instructions directly understood by the computer's central processing unit (CPU). With machine code the above computation (*180.0 ÷ pi*) might look something like this

```
8B542408 83FA0077 06B80000 0000C383
```

Yikes!! Not so easy to understand, eh? While software has been written using machine code for as long as there have been computers, doing this is very labor-intensive and error prone even for the simplest of programs. Hence most software is written using *high-level* languages; these are typically more convenient for writing programs.

High-level languages employ numerous abstractions to reduce and factor out the implementation details of the computer. This enables programmers to focus on a few concepts at a time, and also concentrate on writing program code that solves the actual problem, i.e. the actual algorithms, instructions, and/or *business logic*. High-level languages are designed to make it easier to write code, thereby simplifying both software development and maintenance. However, using high-level programming languages comes with a cost – the programs produced when written with them tends to be larger in size, run slower, and use more memory than programs created using low-level languages. So selecting a programming language involves a tradeoff between ease of use and efficiency.

Ready, Set, Run!
Once you've written a computer program, you probably want to execute it. So you need to know how to run the program what to run it on. For example a program can be executed on a computer or a device. The device itself can be real or simulated. A program can even run inside another program (e.g. a web browser)!

How a program is executed depends upon whether the source code is *compiled* or *interpreted* for execution. Interpretation is a technique whereby another program, an *interpreter*, directly performs the operations specified by the program in order to run it. For example if you read a program and do what it says to do step-by-step, whether that's perform a computation, execute an operation, etc., you are interpreting the program. A common reason to interpret a program is that (compared to a compiler) an interpreter can be an easier tool to develop. Another reason is that an interpreter can monitor what a program tries to do as it runs, to enforce a security policy, perform some specific action like logging, etc.

Compilation is a technique of translating a program written in one language (the "source language") into another (the "object language", typically executable machine code), which means the same thing as the original program. The program used to perform this translation is called a *compiler*. While doing this translation, it is common for a compiler to also have features that attempt to transform the program in ways that will make the executable program run faster. A compiler has many benefits; it enables you to improve program execution performance, write programs that can be run on different computer hardware (compilers often can transform a source program to machine code for multiple types of computers), all while avoiding the overhead of interpreting the source code along the way. Some programming languages, such as Java, have an interpreter along with an optimizing compiler. What this means is that the source code is normally executed using an interpreter, but program code that is executed very often is compiled to improve execution speed.

So there are important differences between compiled and interpreted programs in terms of performance characteristics, flexibility, and other factors. All programming languages have tools to support one or the other approach, and some even support both.

Categories of Programs

There are literally thousands of computer programming languages at present, and new ones continue to be created. Some are specialized, and designed for writing programs for specific domains (like creating/manipulating audio or visual content), while others are general-purpose. Whichever language a program is written in, it probably falls into one of the following categories: 1) system software, 2) application software, or 3) software development tools.

System software is designed to operate the computer hardware and provide a platform for running application software. Common system software includes device drivers, the operating system, user interface software, utility software, and servers.

Device drivers are programs that directly operate and control the computer hardware and peripherals. They function as the interface between a hardware device and either application software or the operating system. Device drivers simplify programming by enabling you to write application code for interacting with devices (disk drives, network devices, etc.) in a uniform way, not dependent on the specific hardware a computer has.

The operating system manages computer resources and enables its components to work together. It also provides a common set of services on which other computer software (including other system software, application software, and development tools) runs. An operating system is found on just about any computer or device. The operating system uses device drivers to interact with the computer hardware.

User interface software provides support for the computer's user interface. Most operating systems provide a graphical user interface (GUI); hence the user interface software includes support for the computer's graphics hardware. Programmers use this software to build the GUI for a program.

Utility software helps to analyze, configure, optimize and maintain the computer. Common examples include anti-virus programs and backup utilities.

Servers are programs that fulfill the requests of users or other programs, performing some operation or task. They are typically accessed over a network. Common examples include a web server or a database.

Application software is designed to help the user perform specific tasks. There are numerous categories of application software; common examples include word processors, graphics software, media players, games, communication utilities, business software, education software, etc.

Software development tools are essentially application software used by programmers to develop and maintain software. Common examples include source code editors, compilers, and debuggers. A source code editor is a program, somewhat like a word processor, that is used to write programs. A compiler is a tool used to translate a program into a format that can be executed by a computer. A debugger is a tool used to find and remove program errors.

There is a hierarchical relationship between these different categories of software. The following diagram depicts this hierarchy.

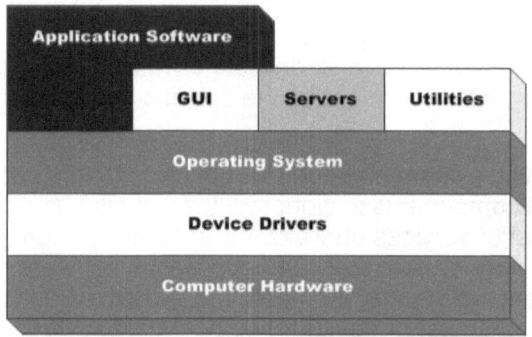

Figure 2. Software Relationships & Hierarchies

As shown in the figure, application software does not interact with the computer hardware directly; rather it obtains computer resources like memory, network access, etc. by using the available operating system services. The operating system software in turn employs device drivers to use the computer hardware. A similar arrangement exists for servers and utilities; they interact directly with the operating system, rather than the device drivers or computer hardware. This type of architecture enables programmers to write software (application software, servers, etc.) that doesn't depend on the specific hardware the computer has, and also enables the operating system to manage the computer's resources effectively.

Summary

In this chapter you received an introduction to computer programming, enough so that you are now pretty familiar with the basic concepts and the types of programs that you can develop with them. You learned about the basic elements of a programming language and the components common to every program. You were introduced to the concept of programming language abstractions and how they make programming easier and more efficient. You also learned about the steps taken to actually execute a program and the many types of programs there are. Next up we'll begin looking at different programming languages in more detail, starting with the Objective-C language.

Chapter 3
Parlez-vous Objective-C?
(Do you speak Objective-C?)

In this chapter we're going to continue our study of programming language fundamentals and start using **Objective-C**, a general purpose, *object-oriented* programming language. So what does that mean, object-oriented? Well, before we begin programming with Objective-C we need to understand what object-oriented programming is, so let's start there.

Object-Oriented Programming

Object-oriented programming, or OOP as it is commonly known, is a style of computer programming that emphasizes the creation and use of *software objects* to write programs. Now you may be asking, what's a software object? Good question; you can think of a software object as a model, in software, of a thing or concept. A software object provides a representation (in software) of the characteristics or attributes of the thing/concept being modeled along with a definition of the things it can do. The attributes (aka its *properties*) that define an object are typically things the object *has or is*; for example if you were modeling a person the set of attributes would include height and weight. The things an object can do (aka its *behaviors*), are generally the actions that it can perform (for a person object this could be things like run, jump, speak, etc.). OK, let's try to clarify this with an example that specifies an object-oriented model of an *atom* (e.g., hydrogen, oxygen, etc.). Now a *very* simplified model of an atom might include the following properties:

- Protons (number of protons of the atom)
- Neutrons (number of neutrons of the atom)
- Electrons (number of electrons of the atom)

We may also want to include some of the things we can do with a software model of an atom:

- **Get Element** (determine the chemical element name [e.g. hydrogen, helium, etc.] of the atom)
- **Get Mass** (determine the atomic mass of the atom)
- **Illustrate** (display a diagram of the atom)
- **Perform Fission** (split the nucleus – very dangerous, perform at your own risk!!)
- **Create** (create an Atom object with the desired number of protons, neutrons, and electrons)

The resulting object-oriented software model for an atom consists of these properties and behaviors.

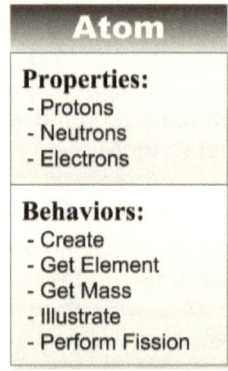

Figure 3. Atom Object

OK, now we have a software model for an atom, so what's next? Well, you get a software object to perform an operation (i.e. a behavior) by sending a message to it with the operation you want performed. For example, if you send the message **Get Element** to an atom object it will determine the chemical element name for the atom and return that information as text (e.g., it might return the text "Hydrogen" or "Helium"). Object-oriented software design is all about creating software objects of this sort and using them to build software applications.

Programmers create networks of interacting objects to implement all sorts of applications.

I mentioned earlier that there are literally thousands of programming languages, and an OOP language is just one of many options for writing programs. So why build this software using objects, why not use another approach? Well, compared to other programming styles, OOP has a variety of benefits and here are just a few of them:

- OOP is a natural tool for modeling things in software, whether they are real-world entities, abstract concepts, and/or processes. This can reduce complexity and make the program structure more clear.
- Because you can create software objects that completely define the properties (i.e. states) and behavior of a thing being modeled, they can be reused in a variety of ways. You can use them to build things that are related and descend from a common parent (let's call this technique *inheritance*), or things that are built up from other objects (let's call this technique *composition*).
- It is easy to make internal changes to an object, as it is self-contained. When an object is designed properly, changes to its implementation do not affect any other part of a program, since the interface that the external world has to the object is specified by its operations (i.e. *methods*).
- Object-oriented software is extensible, meaning that making updates or adding new features doesn't require a complete rewrite of a program. Often, you can update object-oriented software by introducing a few new objects and/or modifying some existing ones.
- As well-defined objects are self-contained and used through a published interface, they can be maintained separately. This makes maintaining programs easier, along with locating and fixing problems. For large programs this feature is especially important.

To put OOP in perspective, much of the software that you use today, whether they are applications that you use on your computers, mobile devices, websites, or in machines, was written using an OOP language. For example, iPhone, iPod, and iPad applications are primarily written in Objective-C. Much of the user interface for Facebook is written with PHP, a programming language that supports OOP. Android applications for your mobile device are written in Java, an OOP language; in fact, Java is used in over 3 billion devices. Many Windows applications are written in Visual Basic or C#, both of which provide extensive support for OOP. This is just a sample of ways that OOP languages are used today; the list goes on and on.

Using OOP

One of the things that make this programming style really powerful is how you can reuse existing objects that you have defined, kind of like a template, to create other objects and thereby build large, complex programs. For example, let's say that you need to create a program that will provide information about the chemical composition of a molecule. It should work like this: the program asks the user for the name of a molecule (let's say water) and it responds with the atomic structure of the molecule (its atoms, in this example hydrogen and oxygen), the ratio of those chemical elements (for water this would be 2 hydrogen atoms to 1 oxygen atom), and displays on the screen an illustration of the molecule.

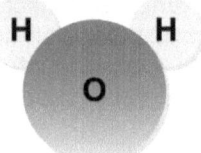

Figure 4. Water Molecule

To write this program, let's create a Molecule object that is a combination of Atom objects.

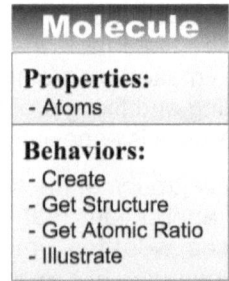

Figure 5. Molecule Object

We can see that a Molecule object is made up of Atom objects, so we can **reuse** the software we built earlier for the Atom object to create the software for the Molecule object. Next, let's suppose that your boss likes this program so much that he tells you to create a program that will provide this information for *biomolecules*. Now, a biomolecule is just a *specialized* type of molecule, so again, we can **reuse** the existing software for the Molecule object as the baseline for creating the software for a Biomolecule object. For us programmers this is very cool, because we can reuse what we have and don't have to write everything from scratch; this enables us to more efficiently create software of almost any level of complexity. Another great thing about this programming style is that it enables you to break down software development tasks into smaller, more manageable programming tasks whose outputs can be assembled together, almost factory-like, to build software systems.

Objective-C at 3,000 Feet

Now that I have thoroughly convinced you of the benefits of OOP, hold on to your saddle, because you're about to begin learning your first programming language!   Mastering any language, much less a programming language, takes time, so I'm not going to mislead you and say that you're going to be fluent at Objective-C after reading this chapter. What I will do here is introduce some of the key elements of the language and how you would use them in a program.

The first thing we want to do is learn some of the basic elements used to create objects using Objective-C. Let's start with the previous example; we want to use Objective-C to create an Atom object that completely specifies its properties and operations. Once we have done that, we can use this specification, kind of like a template or blueprint, to create as many Atom objects as we want. With the Objective-C language you create the specification for an object with an *interface* and a corresponding *implementation*

```
@interface Atom
  Declare Atom properties here
  Declare Atom methods here
@end

@implementation Atom
   Define Atom instance variables here
   Define Atom properties here
   Define Atom methods here
@end
```

So, what are an interface and an implementation? Let's continue with the next section and find out.

Interface
The interface section of an Objective-C object begins with the `@interface` symbol and is terminated with the `@end` symbol. Basically, an interface is where you specify the structure of an object, i.e. its properties and *methods*. In OOP a **property** is a type of variable that represents a characteristic or attribute of the thing/concept you are modeling; as an example some properties of a person object could include height, weight, and gender. For each property of an Objective-C object you specify its name and important data characteristics, such as its data type (e.g., is the property an integer, a decimal number, etc.) and size (is it a small value, a large value, a collection of values, etc.). In the Objective-C language an operation, in other words the things that the object can do, is called a **method**. Hence for each method you specify its name, the inputs for the method, and what data, if any, will be returned as a result of the method being performed.

You can think of an interface like a construction plan; you have to completely specify what the thing you are building has (its properties) and what it can do (its methods) so that you can hand the plan over to someone to build it. With that in mind let's add the necessary detail to completely specify the interface for the Atom object depicted previously; here's the program code:

```
@interface Atom : NSObject
  @property int protons;
  @property int neutrons;
  @property int electrons;

  + (Atom *)createWithProtons:(int)protons
    withNeutrons:(int)neutrons
    withElectrons:(int)electrons;
  - (NSString *)chemicalElement;
  - (float)atomicMass;
  - (void)nuclearFission;
  - (void)illustrate;
@end
```

Yes, I know this may look like Sanskrit or something, so bare
with me here and we'll get through this! Let's start with the
interface, the statement

```
@interface Atom : NSObject
```

begins the interface declaration for an `Atom` object. Now you
probably noticed the funny-looking `:` `NSObject` stuff on this
line; it is saying that an `Atom` object is a child of another object
(`NSObject`). You don't really have to worry about the whole
child concept right now, just understand that this means your
Atom object gets all the functionality provided by `NSObject` (i.e.
its properties and methods) for free (it *inherits* this, remember
our comments on reuse and inheritance in the previous
section?). Now onto the **property** declarations; the code

```
@property int protons;
@property int neutrons;
@property int electrons;
```

says that an Atom object has three variables that represent the
number of protons, neutrons, and electrons it contains. The
`@property` symbol identifies this as a *property declaration*. The
`int` symbol specifies the integer data type for the variable (in
this case the variables are named `protons`, `neutrons`, and
`electrons`). The semicolon (`;`) symbol is used to terminate a
(property declaration) statement, kind of like a period. So we
have specified that an Atom object has 3 properties – an integer
number of protons, neutrons, and electrons. Now let's look at
the **methods** for an Atom object. We'll start with the simplest
looking method, the one listed as

```
- (void)illustrate;
```

The method is named `illustrate`, and its job is to draw an image of an Atom on the screen. The `(void)` symbol indicates that this method doesn't return any data after it runs (it just displays the image on the screen). The `-` symbol at the beginning of the method declaration specifies that this is an *object method* (a + symbol at the beginning of a method declaration specifies a *class method*). Since it's not important right now to know the difference between class methods and object methods, we'll leave this one alone. As before, the semicolon symbol is used to terminate the statement. The remaining methods have the same syntax but differ in the details, for example the method

```
- (float)atomicMass;
```

Computes and returns a decimal number value for the atomic mass of the Atom. The method

```
- (NSString *)chemicalElement;
```

Returns the chemical element name for the atom as text (in Objective-C speak, as an `NSString *`). The most complex method declaration

```
+ (Atom *)createWithProtons:(int)protons
  withNeutrons:(int)neutrons
  withElectrons:(int)electrons;
```

Actually creates and returns an Atom object. The number of protons, neutrons, and electrons that it should have are integer values that are provided when you make the object perform the method.

And that's it; we have now completely specified the structure for an Atom object! We can give this interface to a programmer and have him/her actually build an Atom object based on this structure, and that's where the object *implementation* comes into the picture.

Implementation

The implementation section of an Objective-C object begins with the `@implementation` symbol and is terminated with a `@end` symbol. Where the interface section specifies the structure of an object, the implementation contains program code that specifies its instance variables, defines the properties, and performs the logic for each method. Instance variables, like properties, are data with a specific type and size. They differ from properties in that they are neither publically visible nor accessible. You would typically store data that defines the internal state of an object in one or more instance variables. The implementation of the `illustrate` method for an Atom would look like this.

```
@implementation Atom

    - (void)illustrate
    {
      Insert Code to draw an Atom object on the screen here
    }
@end
```

The bulk of your work will be writing this software to implement algorithms, carry out actions, create and use other objects to do the same, and in effect anything required to completely perform the requested operation. Let's demonstrate this with the `Molecule` object. Recall that it is composed of one or more Atom objects. Given that you have already implemented the code for Atom objects (remember we are reusing the Atom object software, one of the great features of OOP), the code you would implement for a Molecule object's `getStructure` method should do the following

- Get the chemical element name for each Atom object; you would do this by performing the `chemicalElement` method for the Atom. This would return in text an appropriate chemical element name, such as "Hydrogen", "Helium", "Oxygen", etc.
- Use the information received from calling the `chemicalElement` method on each Atom to create and return a text phrase which names the overall atomic structure of the molecule (e.g., for a water molecule it should return the answer "Hydrogen, Oxygen").

And that's it! This is how programmers develop a network of interacting objects to implement Objective-C applications.

Object Messaging
Now that we know how to build an object in Objective-C, let's look at the code we write to make an object perform an operation. After all, in the previous example the implementation

for the Molecule `getStructure` method has to retrieve the chemical element name for each of its Atoms (i.e., perform the `chemicalElement` method). You may recall that I said you have to send a message to an object to get it to perform an operation, so that's what we want to look at here.

You send a message to an object by specifying the object that should receive the message (i.e., the *receiver*), the name of the method that you want it to perform, along with any value(s) you need to provide to the method. This process is very similar to real-world interactions. For example your son/daughter knows how to perform the "make your bed" operation, so if you want this operation performed, you send him/her (the *receiver*) this message and it should happen, at least in theory! Back to programming, let's say that you have created an Atom object named `hydrogen` and you want to display this object on the screen; you do this by sending the following message

```
[hydrogen illustrate];
```

And the code that you've written to draw the atom on the screen (as shown in Figure 4) is run. Or let's say that you want to get the value for the atomic mass of our object and save it in a variable named `hmass`, you would send the following message

```
float hmass = [hydrogen atomicMass];
```

and this code does just that. As a more complex example, let's say that you want to create a new atom model, this time of oxygen, you would send the message

```
Atom *oxAtom = [Atom createWithProtons:8
  withNeutrons:8 withElectrons:8];
```

This creates a new Atom object (that models the oxygen atom) and assigns this object to a variable named `oxAtom`. From these examples we can see that, in general, the code for sending a message to an object looks like this

```
[receiver methodNamePart1:value1
  methodNamePart2:value2, …];
```

where the receiver, method name parts, and input values are provided in order, and the whole expression is surrounded by square brackets followed by a terminating semicolon. Also note that the name part and corresponding input value are separated by a colon symbol.

Objective-C Key Features

This has been a pretty detailed chapter and we have covered many new concepts. To recap, let's summarize some of the key features of OOP and how they are supported in the Objective-C programming language.

OOP

Object-Oriented Programming is a style of programming for which the chief building blocks of a program (data, instructions for manipulating data) are structured as **objects**. An object is a programming entity that is made up of both data and the operations (methods) for manipulating this data. The operations that can be performed on an object include accessing and/or updating its data elements, performing computations (e.g. implementing algorithms, etc.), and invoking operations on other objects. An object-oriented program executes its logic by creating object instances and invoking the desired operations on these objects. In a nutshell, object-oriented software can be viewed as a collection of interacting objects.

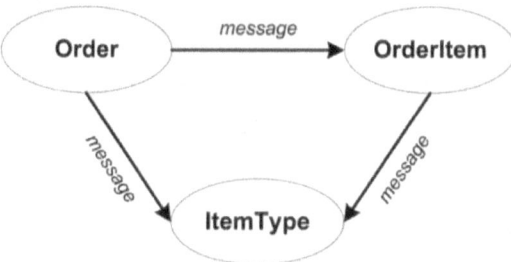

Figure 6. Object Interaction

You develop object-oriented software by structuring application logic as *classes*. A class is a blueprint for creating objects. OOP simplifies the design and development of classes through concepts like encapsulation, inheritance, and polymorphism.

Class

An Objective-C class specification is primarily defined with an interface and its corresponding implementation. The interface specifies the structure of an object, i.e. its instance variables, properties and methods. The implementation contains program code that actually defines the properties and implements the logic for each method. A class specification may also include *protocol* and/or *category* class elements. A protocol is a special type of (common) interface that can be implemented by multiple classes. A category is used to add new functionality (i.e. new properties and methods) to an existing class.

Encapsulation

In OOP encapsulation refers to the grouping together of data and operations on that data, along with the ability to restrict access to some of an object's data and/or operations. Objective-C provides support for data encapsulation. The interface, protocol, category, and implementation class elements are used to provide a well-defined specification for a class that combines all of its data and operations. Objective-C also includes several mechanisms that can be used to restrict/prevent direct access to data; thereby making software development and update easier.

Inheritance

Inheritance is a feature of OOP that enables the development of new classes based on previously defined classes. This new class inherits the state (data) and behavior (methods) of the pre-existing class. The new class is termed the subclass (or derived class) while the pre-existing class is referred to as the parent class. The relationship between a parent class and a subclass is a hierarchy; inheritance makes it possible to create hierarchies of classes, each of which is based on a parent class. Objective-C supports single inheritance of both attributes and behavior, meaning a class can have only one parent.

Polymorphism

The word *polymorphism* is derived from the Greek language and means *having several different forms*. In OOP polymorphism refers to a programming language's ability to process objects differently depending on their data type or class, thereby allowing values of different data types to be processed with a uniform interface. Objective-C supports polymorphism through class hierarchies and its dynamic runtime.

Object Messaging

Objective-C object messaging is the mechanism used for communication between objects. In effect, an Objective-C object *(the sender)* sends a message to a receiving object *(the receiver)* and the receiver uses the message to perform the corresponding operation, returning a result if required. The exact method call (both the object type for the receiver and the method to perform) is determined during program execution.

Dynamic Runtime

Objective-C is a dynamic programming language; whenever possible it does things dynamically during program execution, rather than statically prior to running the program. The dynamic runtime features include message sending, dynamically providing a method implementation, dynamically determining the type of an object, and dynamically loading code and resources as they are needed. These features make it possible to write Objective-C programs that are both very flexible and can also evolve during execution.

Summary

In this chapter you learned about Objective-C and object-oriented programming and began looking at program code in depth. OOP emphasizes the creation and use of software objects to write programs. It is one of the most common styles of programming in use today and is supported by numerous programming languages. Objective-C, an OOP language, is the primary programming language used to develop applications that run on both Apple computers (Mac Pro, MacBook, etc.) and devices (iPod, iPad, iPhone). It is flexible, easy to learn and use, and generates very efficient code. The Objective-C language, combined with the tools and software provided by Apple make this a great platform for software development. If you want to go further and learn Objective-C in depth, there are numerous books available. You can also find plenty of information on the web and helpful users groups. If you would like to get started with Objective-C programming in a hurry, you're also welcome to check out the book **Core Objective-C** *in 24 Hours,* available at http://www.motupresse.com.

Chapter 4
Language Types

OK, so far we have covered the basics of computer programming, OOP and Objective-C. Soon we'll dive into other topics like web programming, mobile apps, graphics and animation, game programming, and more. In fact, in the upcoming chapters we are going to be writing our own programs! Before we do that though, this is a good time to learn more about the different types of programming languages and how they are used; after all, Objective-C is not the only one available. So, the question is, how do we choose which language to use for writing a program? To answer that, let's spend a little more time getting familiar with the different types of programming languages, their common characteristics, and key features.

Common Characteristics

Just like natural languages, programming languages can be grouped according to common characteristics. These include qualities like the abstractions it provides and the programming style(s) it supports. We'll learn about these characteristics next.

Abstraction Levels

By definition, an abstraction removes underlying, unwanted details in order to reduce complexity and reveal the original thing or entity. Programming languages provide abstractions that enable you to write programs that solve the actual problem (e.g. performing a computation, controlling a device, etc.) without having to consider the specifics of the computer hardware on which the program executes. They are designed to support, at a minimum, control abstractions (control flow, for the execution of instructions) and data abstractions (for data management). Now we'll look at an example to clarify what all of this means in practice.

Example: Fibonacci Numbers

What we want to do here is show how abstractions impact the program code you develop. Let's do this by presenting an example problem and then a corresponding solution (i.e. program) in several programming languages (each of which has a different level of support for abstractions).

In mathematics Fibonacci numbers follow the sequence

```
0, 1, 1, 2, 3, 5, 8, 13, 21, 34, 55, 89, ...
```

By definition, the first two numbers of the sequence are 0 and 1, and each subsequent number is the sum of the previous two. Now let's say that we want to write a program that gets the value of a number in the Fibonacci sequence; in other words if you request the 8th element in the sequence (where the 0th element has a value of **0**) the program should return the value 21. The equation for computing a *Fibonacci* number is

$$F_n = F_{n-1} + F_{n-2}$$

Where F_n is the number you are trying to compute and F_{n-1}, F_{n-2} are the two previous numbers. Thus if the first two numbers are 0 and 1, the second number is 0 + 1 = 1, the third number is 1 + 1 = 2, the fourth number is 1 + 2 = 3, etc. So our job is to write a program that implements this equation, taking the input Fibonacci element and returning the value of the corresponding number.

Machine Code Implementation

Machine code has **no** abstractions; thus programs written with machine code can be processed directly by the computer without translation. Here is the Fibonacci number equation implemented as machine code for a particular type of computer (Note, these binary machine instructions are written with hexadecimal representations).

```
8B542408 83FA0077 06B80000 0000C383
FA027706 B8010000 00C353BB 01000000
B9010000 008D0419 83FA0376 078BD98B
C84AEBF1 5BC3
```

Does this program look anything like the equation? Can you imagine having to write program code like this to perform even simple computations or operations, much less more complex ones?

Low-Level Language Implementation
Low-level languages are primarily *assembly* languages that provide basic support for abstractions. An assembly language is specific to a computer's hardware architecture. Thus, while assembly is not machine code, to use it the programmer must still understand the computer hardware. Once you have written a program using assembly language, a tool called an *assembler* is used to transform this into the machine code executed by the computer. Assembly language data abstractions are used to define the type and length of data. The control abstractions include the ability to use *mnemonics* (instead of binary machine codes) to represent machine operations, the grouping of sequences of machine instructions as reusable *macros*, and the definition of *directives* that can execute variable instructions at assembly time. Here is the Fibonacci number equation programmed written in assembly language.

```
fibonacci:
  mov edx, [esp+8]
  cmp edx, 0
  ja @f
  mov eax, 0
  ret

@@:
cmp edx, 2
ja @f
mov eax, 1
ret

@@:
push ebx
mov ebx, 1
mov ecx, 1

@@:
     lea eax, [ebx+ecx]
     cmp edx, 3
     jbe @f
     mov ebx, ecx
     mov ecx, eax
     dec edx
jmp @b

@@:
pop ebx
ret
```

Again, the assembly code doesn't look anything like the actual equation, but at least we're starting to see terms that correspond more to a natural language (for example, mov is the symbol for a machine operation code which instructs the computer to perform a *move operation,* i.e. to copy data from one location to another). Assembly languages also have constructs that enable you to control program flow, execute specific portions of code repeatedly, and perform conditional logic. A program written in assembly language can be made to run very quickly, and use very little memory. However, assembly is still difficult to use, since it just provides a thin veneer over the underlying computer hardware and the language itself doesn't correspond to the problem domain.

In addition, as with machine code, assembly language is specific to the computer hardware, thus the program code must be rewritten to run on another type of computer.

High-Level Language Implementation

High-level languages have numerous abstractions that are designed to factor out the details of the computer and simplify programming.   Code written using a high-level language is translated into executable machine code with a compiler or executed with an interpreter (see **Ready, Set, Run** section in Chapter 2). Compilers for high-level languages are typically designed to generate programs that can be executed on multiple types of computers and platforms; this greatly increases application portability (likewise interpreters are implemented for multiple types of computers and platforms). The abstractions support many types of control flows, data structures, programming styles, and other useful programming features. Additionally high-level languages often include one or more software libraries that can be used to simplify program development. Here is the Fibonacci number equation programmed in Objective-C.

```
-  (unsigned int) fibonacci: (unsigned int)
   element
{
  if (element <= 0)
  {
    // if 0th element return a value of 0
    return 0;
  }
  else if (element <= 2)
  {
    // if 1st or 2nd element return value of 1
    return 1;
  }
  else
  {
    unsigned int fi = 0;
    unsigned int fi1 = 1;
    unsigned int fi2 = 1;
    while (YES)
    {
      // loop to sum value of elements
      fi = fi1 + fi2;
      if (element <= 3)
      {
        // added all elements, return value
        return fi;
      }
      fi1 = fi2;
      fi2 = fi;
      element = element - 1;
    }
  }
}
```

This code is a significant improvement over assembly code in terms of readability, hence it is easier to use and maintain. It defines and uses multiple control flows and data types. Finally, programs written using high-level languages, such as Objective-C, can be run on multiple computers and platforms.

So, given the benefits of high-level languages, why would you ever want to use a low-level language? After all, the code you write with a high-level language is much easier to understand, and your programs can also be compiled to run on multiple computer platforms. Well, there are still some scenarios where low-level assembly languages are used. An assembly language allows you to control the computer as precisely as you can, as assembly instructions operate directly on the computer hardware, and programs written in assembly are translated directly into machine code. So you have more precise control, and can potentially improve program performance and reduce memory usage. However, as was previously noted, programming in a low-level language is more difficult, requires a higher level of skill, and results in programs that are less portable and more difficult to maintain. The types of applications where this potential performance gain may warrant the use of assembly language include programs that have very limited resources (e.g. devices with limited memory), very high performance applications (graphics-oriented games, etc.), and real-time applications.   The following diagram captures the progression of abstraction levels for programming languages.

Abstractions	Key Characteristics	Example Languages
None	Machine instructions Binary Directly executed on CPU	Intel IA-32 Instruction Set
Low-Level	Assembly language Text format instructions Simple abstractions (macros, data types) Assembler translates to machine code	Motorola 68K Assembly
Medium-Level	Some natural language elements More abstractions (subroutines, data structures, etc.) More portable across platforms	ANSI C
High-Level	Potentially numerous natural language elements Numerous abstractions Runtime components for resource management	Objective-C, Java,

Table 1. Abstraction Levels

Programming Styles
OK, you now have a good understanding of programming abstractions, but do you have enough information to know

what language to use to write a given program? As you know, the choice of programming language can have a significant impact on the ease and efficiency with which you write a program. Another key factor in choosing a programming language is the type of problem you are trying to solve and how well it maps to the programming language(s) you are considering. Should the program describe *how* to accomplish something (i.e. by a sequence of commands)? Should it describe *what* to accomplish (i.e. the logic of a computation, or what it is)? Is the program flow sequential, or is it determined by internal/external events? Should a program be able to perform many operations simultaneously, or just one at a time? These types of considerations greatly influence the programming *style(s)* that you use to develop a program.

A programming style (aka, *paradigm*) can be considered the *approach*, i.e. the techniques and styles, used to write a program. Its key characteristics include the concepts and abstractions used to represent the basic elements of a program (such as its variables, methods, objects, etc.), and the steps that make up a computation (assignment, evaluation, continuations, data flows, etc.). For example, OOP is a programming paradigm that employs the object abstraction to represent both data and the operations that can be performed on data. Many programming languages support two or more approaches (i.e. paradigms) for software development; often one for developing small programs and another for developing larger programs. Multiple languages support some common paradigms, for example many languages (such as Objective-C, Java, PHP, etc.) support OOP. Several common programming paradigms are:

- **Declarative** programming focuses on describing what something is by identifying its attributes and characteristics, defining its mathematical relations, specifying its rules, etc. A programming expression written with a declarative programming language is *referentially transparent;* this means that it always produces the same result for a given set of inputs and doesn't modify the state of another part of the program.

- **Functional** programming is a type of declarative programming that emphasizes the creation of computer programs as referentially transparent mathematical functions.
- **Imperative** programming defines a solution through sequences of commands for the computer to perform. In contrast to functional programming, imperative programming defines a program in terms of its state (i.e. memory). In addition, unlike declarative programming it can modify state.
- **Structured** programming aims to improve the clarity, quality, and development time of a program by making extensive use of program flow structures. OOP is a style of structured programming that combines data with the operations you can perform on that data.

Once you know the type of program you want to develop, then you can more readily determine the programming paradigm(s) for the program and then use a programming language that supports that paradigm. For example, what type of language would be a good choice for creating an electronic library card catalog? Since a card catalog provides information on a book such as its name, description, location in the library, etc. (in other words *descriptive* information), then a language that supports declarative programming would be a good choice. If you need to create a program that solves a given set of linear equations for a set of inputs (i.e., mathematical functions), then a language that supports functional programming would be appropriate. On the other hand, if you need to create a program that will be used to perform inventory management for a library (place orders, support different types of inventory items [e.g. books, electronic media], track shipping, etc.) then an OOP language might be appropriate. In summary, consider choosing your programming language based on the programming paradigm(s) it supports.

Language Generations

The types of programming languages created have evolved over time, beginning with machine code up to the present day. Currently we can distinguish five generations of programming languages; by generation we don't mean the age of a programming language, rather this provides a relative indication of when the different categories of programming languages began to be developed. For example, the initial 1st generation languages were developed before the initial 2nd generation languages, etc. Some of the characteristics typical for each generation of programming languages are described here:

- **First Generation Languages** are machine languages. Programs written with these languages are directly executed by the computer, and thus require no translation. Machine instructions are typically written with binary notation. As we saw earlier in this chapter, writing machine code requires extensive knowledge of both the computer hardware and the machine operation codes.
- **Second Generation Languages** are assembly languages. They employ simple abstractions, such as symbols to represent machine operation codes, memory locations, registers, and other parts of an instruction. These languages typically use an assembler to translate assembly instruction symbols (aka *mnemonics*) into machine code, and resolve symbolic names for memory locations and other entities. Assembly language programming requires extensive knowledge of the CPU and instruction set. As with first generation languages, assembly language programs are not portable to different computers.
- **Third Generation Languages** are characterized by compiled code and machine independence, while still retaining good performance. These languages feature abstractions that enable more structured programming, facilitate reuse of blocks of code through subroutines, and support numerous data types.
- **Fourth Generation Languages** have even more abstractions that effectively hide the details of the computer hardware while supporting high-level specifications. Many of these languages are specific to a problem domain and are designed for building specific types programs (for example, database languages).
- **Fifth Generation Languages** are based around solving problems using constraints defined in the

program, rather than implementing algorithms in a program. These languages denote the properties, or logic, of a solution, rather than how the solution is reached. In the past fifth generation languages were mainly used for artificial intelligence research, but are now finding more use with other classes of problems.

Summary

There are thousands of programming languages, and new ones are being created all the time. Hence it can be difficult to determine the best language for writing a program. In this chapter we have examined several characteristics that can help you with your selection. You now understand the abstraction level of a programming language, and how it affects different aspects of a computer program. You also know how to choose a programming language based on the paradigm(s) it supports. Of course, your existing knowledge and experience with programming languages, the supporting tools you have available, and other external factors will also factor in your decision.

OK, now that you know how to choose a programming language, perhaps it's a good time to take a break and give your brain a well-deserved rest. In the next chapter, you're going to begin writing your own web pages!

Chapter 5
Welcome to My World (Wide Web)

In the first few chapters you have learned a lot about computer programming languages, and now have a good understanding of them and how to choose a language for writing your own programs. That makes this a great time to begin writing your own code! Let's start by creating some web pages with HTML (HyperText Markup Language), the main **document markup language** of the web. But wait a minute; haven't we been learning about programming languages, what's a *markup language*? OK, so let's clear this one up before we move on.

Mark This One Up

Now technically speaking markup languages are not programming languages; you can think of one as a set of symbols and rules used to provide information about text. For example, you've probably submitted a document (like an essay) to a teacher and he/she returned it to you with markup for corrections (using symbols indicating recommended grammar and punctuation changes and the like). You then process the document (make the corrections) and submit a new version for review. This illustrates how document markup languages are used; to *markup* a document for some (additional) processing. What the processing will be depends upon the markup language and the tool(s) used to process the markup document.

Using HTML

HTML is used for marking up text to define its *structure* and *meaning*. This means defining things like the sections of a page, its paragraphs, images, audio and/or video content, links to other pages, etc. Think of it like this: you create all of your content for a web page in one or more text files, and then mark it up with HTML. Since many applications (e.g. web browsers, etc.) support HTML, they will know how to process your HTML document(s) and present its content, whether that be displaying it on a monitor, printing it on paper, performing a text-to-speech conversion, etc.

So, you create an HTML document (i.e., a *web page*) and store it in a place where it can be accessed by a browser. If you open your browser and input the *URL* for the page, it will be displayed in the browser window; pretty cool eh? OK, now that you understand the process, it's time to look at some other important details that you need to understand in order to create your own web pages, let's start with how HTML documents are organized.

Structure of an HTML Document

HTML documents have the following structure

DOCTYPE Declaration
HTML Section
- *Head Section (optional)*
- *Body Section*

The *DOCTYPE Declaration* specifies the version of HTML that the page is written in. The declaration is written as follows

`<!DOCTYPE` ***type***`>`

Notice that the declaration begins with the text `<!DOCTYPE`, then the variable ***type***, which indicates the version of HTML the web page is written in. The declaration concludes with a > character. For example, the declaration

`<!DOCTYPE html>`

says that the page is written in HTML version 5. A DOCTYPE declaration should always be provided at the beginning of a web page.

The *HTML Section* contains the bulk of an HTML document. All other document sections (specifically the Head and Body

sections) are contained within the HTML section. The optional
Head Section contains information about the document and any
additional information used to process the document. This
includes things like the document title, links to other documents,
and additional processing instructions. The *Body Section*
contains the actual document content. So, a minimal web page
would be the following

```
<!DOCTYPE html>
<html>
  <body>
    Hello, World!
  </body>
</html>
```

Let's translate this. The first line is the DOCTYPE declaration;
we've seen this before. The text "Hello, World!" is the document
content. Everything else is markup for defining the document
structure. Now that you understand HTML document structure
let's look at the markup in more detail.

Markup with HTML Elements

Each HTML element consists of a **begin tag**, optional **attributes**
and **content,** and an **end tag** (if necessary). A begin tag
contains the following parts in order:

1. A "<" character
2. The element's tag name
3. Optional attributes
4. An optional "/" character (only if there is no content)
5. A ">" character

For example, the HTML section is marked by the *root element*;
`<html>` is the start tag for this section (its tag name is `html`).
You saw this in the example web page right after the DOCTYPE
declaration. An end tag contains the following parts in order:

1. A "<" character
2. A "/" character
3. The element's tag name
4. A ">" character

In the example you see the HTML

```
<html>
  <body>
    Hello, World!
  </body>
</html>
```

Notice that the Body section is contained within the HTML section, and that the start tags and end tags are lined up so that they are **not** interleaved (the tags are balanced, kind of like a pyramid, so that the start and end tags are paired). Also note that the contents of an element are placed between its start and end tags, e.g. the text Hello, World! is placed between the Body section start and end tags.

There are over 100 tags in HTML 5, the latest version of the language. They are used to define the structure of basic text, lists, forms, links, phrases, images and objects, audio, video, and other document elements. There are plenty of online resources that document the complete set of HTML tags, we'll use a few of them ourselves when we create our first web page.

The tag **attributes** provide additional information about an HTML element. They are specified as key/value pairs within a start tag, for instance in the following example the paragraph tag (p) is modified with an attribute to specify a unique identifier (key id1) for the paragraph element.

```
<p id="id1">
  This is a paragraph of text.
</p>
```

As shown in the example, the attribute key (i.e. name) is followed by an equals sign and then a value (in parentheses); if there are multiple attributes for an element they are separated by commas.

All right, now that we understand the basic structure of web pages, let's revisit the example we presented earlier.

```
<!DOCTYPE html>
<html>
  <body>
    Hello, World!
  </body>
</html>
```

This is a simple yet complete HTML document, as it specifies the version of HTML being used (HTML 5), the HTML section, and the Body section. The HTML section is defined with the root element markup, and the Body section is defined with the body element markup. The document content is contained within the body element. Now if you created a file (let's call it *hello.html*) and typed the above document into the file, it would be a valid web page that you could display with your web browser.

Creating Your First Web Page

All right, that's enough of an introduction, now it's time to roll up your sleeves and create some web pages! You will need a computer that allows you to create and save files, and also a web browser; for these examples I will use the Firefox web browser. Also keep in mind the recommendations from **Chapter 1**: 1) Proper syntax, 2) Check your work, 3) One step at a time.

Basic Content

Imagine that you want to create web page that will display in your browser

Greetings, Earthlings!
This is my first web page.

Let's call this web page `hello.html`; you can choose another name if you prefer, as long as the page name ends in either *.html* or *.htm* (these file name endings tell the browser that this is an HTML document). Create the new file and save it on your hard disk (remember where you saved it!). Note that some computers tack an extra suffix onto the file name (for example they might save the file you created as `hello.html.txt`). If this is the case, rename the file to `hello.html` before continuing.

Now open the file and add the following markup, remembering to save the file when you're done.

```
<!DOCTYPE html>
<html>
  <body>
    Greetings, Earthlings!
    This is my first web page.
  </body>
</html>
```

OK, based on what we've learned so far this looks like a perfectly valid HTML document, so let's display it in our browser and see what it looks like. Start your browser and open your new web page. In Firefox you open a web page by selecting the **Open File ...** command from the **File** menu then finding and opening your file (`hello.html`) from where you saved it. On your browser you'll probably see something like this

Greetings Earthlings! This is my first web page.

Great, the page displays! However, it doesn't quite look the way we wanted it; for one thing the two sentences are on the same line, why is that? The reason is that we haven't added any markup to the text to tell the browser how to display it. Without the proper markup or presentation instructions browsers just display text using their default settings, like using their default font selections, ignoring new lines, etc. So let's update our page to change this, the first thing we want to do is have the first sentence (**Greetings, Earthlings!**) on one line and the second sentence below it. Let's use the HTML *paragraph* element to do this, edit your web page as follows (remember to save your updated page!)

```
<!DOCTYPE html>
<html>
  <body>
    <p>Greetings, Earthlings!</p>
    This is my first web page.
  </body>
</html>
```

The first sentence has been marked up with the paragraph element (see the `p` start and end tags surrounding it?). The browser reads this markup and will now display this text a separate paragraph, with some space following the text. Let's reload the page in the browser; it should look something like this

Greetings Earthlings!
This is my first web page.

OK, that's progress. Our page is looking pretty good now, but there's something else that doesn't appear quite right, we would like the letters of the first sentence to appear larger than those of the second, can we achieve this with markup? Yes we can, let's edit our page again to use an HTML *heading* element as follows

```
<!DOCTYPE html>
<html>
  <body>
    <h3>Greetings, Earthlings!</h3>
    This is my first web page.
  </body>
</html>
```

The heading elements are used to define headings for a web page. By default a browser displays a heading on a separate line (with space below it), and with a different font size. There are six HTML heading tags (h1 to h6) with **h1** corresponding to the most important heading (it has the largest relative font size) and **h6** the least important (it has the smallest font size). Here we chose **h3**; feel free to choose a different heading tag to vary the font size if you wish. Let's reload our page again; it should now look something like this

Greetings, Earthlings!
This is my first web page.

Perfect, we have created the web page of our dreams! Everything looks good and we could stop here, but let's go a little further to add a finishing touch to our page and also learn some more HTML. If you have been paying close attention when displaying your page in the browser you may have noticed that it doesn't have a title. In Firefox this means that you don't see a title displayed in the browser tab, instead you see the file name. Now we would like the page to display a proper title; we can do this using some more markup.

You provide the title for a web page with markup text that you place in the Head section. I mentioned earlier that the Head section is where you put optional information on a web page, and the page title is one of those things. Let's create the title now and name it **My First Web Page**; edit your web page and add the following markup

```
<!DOCTYPE html>
<html>
  <head>
    <title>My First Web Page</title>
  </head>
  <body>
    <h3>Greetings, Earthlings!</h3>
    This is my first web page.
  </body>
</html>
```

The *head* element (the `head` start and end tags) is used to define the markup for the Head section. Within this section we added the markup for the title page (the *title* element). Now if you open the your web page on your browser, you will see

Greetings, Earthlings!
This is my first web page.

with the title **My First Web Page**. Bravo, great job, that wasn't so bad, was it? You have created your first web page; you can now take a bow!

Presentation and Behavior
You did a great job creating your first web page, but let's be honest; the page is pretty plain. So, how do we make it snazzier? For example, let's say that we want it to display the current date and also use a different font for some of the text. To do this, we need to incorporate some other technologies that will enable us to modify what the page looks like and how it behaves.

It was mentioned early on in this chapter that HTML is used to provide structure and meaning to a document. But to take your web pages to the next level you need to use, believe it or not, *additional programming languages!* Now you may be wondering, and rightly so, why more languages, we've already learned several them so far, isn't this enough? Well, computer languages, whether they are of the programming kind, markup kind, or some other type, are designed to be concise and focus on a specific problem set. For web pages, you want to control their structure, presentation, and behavior, hence the use of specific languages for each of these areas. You already know that HTML is the language for defining the structure of a web page. Now we'll look at two new languages, one to control how a web page looks (Cascading Style Sheets) and one to control its behavior (JavaScript).

Cascading Style Sheets

Cascading Style Sheets (CSS) is a *style sheet* language that is commonly used to specify the presentation of HTML documents. The way it works is that you create a set of rules that specify formatting and presentation properties (for example colors, fonts, document layout, etc.) and which HTML element(s) the rules apply to. You then add these rules to the web page elements on which you want to apply these rules, and the browser will use them to present the web page appropriately. Now we will not dive into the details around CSS and discuss the numerous style elements it supports, but what we will do here is create a simple example of how it's used. Open up your web page (hello.html) and make the following edits marked in **bold**.

```
<!DOCTYPE HTML>
<html>
  <head>
    <title>My First Web Page</title>
    <style type="text/css">
      p {color:blue;}
    </style>
  </head>
  <body>
    <h1>Greetings, Earthlings!</h1>
    <p>This is my first web page.</p>
  </body>
</html>
```

We just used the CSS *color* property to set the color of the paragraph text to blue. Notice that the style is defined in the Head section within the *style* element (between the style start and end tags) and says that any HTML marked up with the paragraph element should have the color blue. Now if you open your web page on your browser, you'll see

Greetings, Earthlings!

This is my first web page.

Great, now you have a basic idea of how CSS is used to control the presentation of web pages. Let's tackle JavaScript next.

JavaScript
JavaScript is the most widely used programming language for the web. It is used for controlling the behavior of web pages, specifically for making them more interactive. JavaScript code can be implemented to enable your web pages to react to events (for example when you click on a web page button), dynamically modify elements on a web page, validate input data, and a host of other things. JavaScript supports object-oriented programming and is also used for general-purpose application development.

What we're going to do here is update our web page to include some JavaScript that will display the current date and time. Open the page and make the following edits marked in **bold**

```
<!DOCTYPE HTML>
<html>
  <head>
    <title>My First Web Page</title>
    <style type="text/css">
      p {color:blue;}
    </style>
  </head>
  <body>
    <h1>Greetings, Earthlings!</h1>
    <p id="now"></p>
    <script type="text/javascript">
      var time = new Date();
      document.getElementById("now").innerHTML=
        "The current time is " + time;
    </script>
  </body>
</html>
```

Now let's carefully go over these edits. The JavaScript code is placed between the *script* element tags. Basically what it does is get the current date and time (by creating a `Date` object, remember JavaScript supports OOP) and displaying that as text between the paragraph element tags. As there can be multiple paragraphs in a page we create and use an attribute for the paragraph (`id`, set to a value of *now*) to display the date and time in the correct paragraph. Now if you reload the web page on your browser, you'll see

Greetings, Earthlings!

The current time is Mon Feb 27 2012 19:19:24 GMT-0800 (Pacific Standard Time)

And that's it; you've created a web page that displays a greeting along with the current date and time!

Serving Up Your Pages

So far we have been displaying our web pages by using the **Open File ...** command. Now you may be wondering, why aren't we typing in a web address to view our page? You know, opening a web page by entering something in your browser like http://motupresse.com/hello.html? That's a good question; the answer has to do with how we surf the web and how web resources (like pages, media files, etc.) are made available online. Normally you access a web resource from a browser by entering its address (i.e., its *URL*). A Uniform Resource Locator (URL) is a string of characters used to identify a resource accessible over the internet. The first part of the URL (in this example http://motupresse.com/) specifies the Internet address of a *website*, a set of related web pages and other resources and last part (hello.html) the path name of the resource at the website. A website runs on a program called a web server. So, in order to make web pages accessible over the Internet they need to be hosted on a website (e.g. stored in a location accessible to a web server). There are numerous companies online that will setup a website for you to host your web pages. The process is documented online at the website of each web hosting service provider.

HTML Key Features

HTML is the foundation for creating web pages.

- HTML is used for organizing page content.
- CSS is used to control a web page's visual presentation (appearance and layout).
- JavaScript is used to add dynamic elements and behavior to a page.

HTML elements consist of markup tags surrounding web page content.

- Opening tag, content, closing tag.
- An opening tag may have attributes that provide additional information about an element.

There are numerous tag types for specifying a document's elements.

- Structural tags describe the purpose of the page content (html, head, body, etc.).
- Basic text tags organize and/or describe the appearance of page content (br, p, h1-h6, etc.). Note that in general, the appearance of a web page should be controlled using CSS.
- Advanced text tags provide advanced formatting of page content (table, list, etc.).
- Form tags are used to create and process input forms (form, input, select, etc.).
- Hypertext tags links a page to other documents (anchor, etc.).

HTML 5 is the latest version of the language, it adds many new features.

- New tags
- Multimedia (audio and video)
- 2D/3D graphics
- CSS3 support
- Local data storage
- Local database

Summary

Well, this has been a lot of fun. You are now officially a programmer, at least as far as I'm concerned (although I don't know if you should update your resume quite yet!). Obviously there's a lot more to this if you want to create truly interactive, feature-rich web sites. Just know that you can find out practically anything you want to know about web programming by browsing online and/or looking into the many books on the subject.

OK, now you may want to take a short break, because in the upcoming chapters things are going to get even better; we'll look into creating mobile applications, computer graphics, games, and more. However before we do that, I think that it would be a good idea to diverge a bit and learn a thing or two about inner workings of the computer! Don't worry, it will be a helpful yet painless encounter, so when you're ready turn the page and we'll get started.

Chapter **6**
Dissecting the Machine

We are really beginning to find our *inner geek* now, so this is a great time to explore a subject that we have pretty much avoided so far, and that's computer hardware itself. Now, I know that it isn't strictly necessary to understand how a computer works, as the programming and markup languages we have used so far abstract away those details. However, it can be useful to have a general awareness of the major components of computers and how they work together, whether you are looking to buy a new computer or just want to understand how your programs run. So, let's open this thing up and see what's inside!

How it Works

If you removed the enclosure for a computer and looked at the *circuit board* that holds its main components, you might see something like the following.

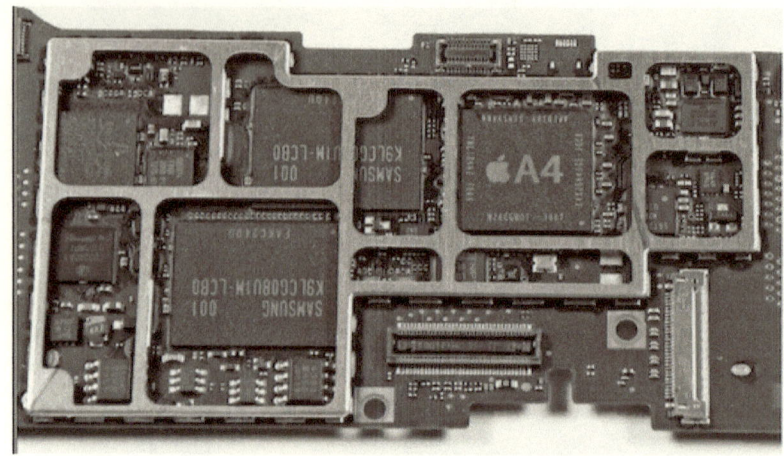

Figure 7. Computer Circuit Board

A computer circuit board contains one or more processing units for executing instructions, memory used to store programs and data, and circuitry for communicating with peripherals. Secondary storage may be onboard or located externally.

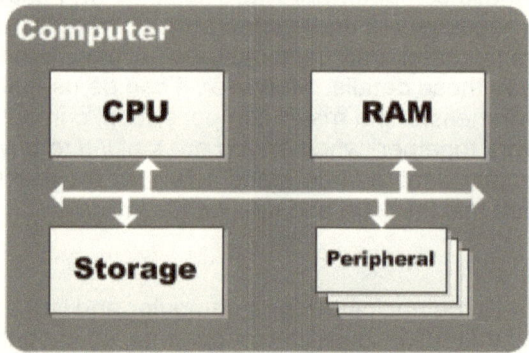

Figure 8. Computer Internals

- Central Processing Unit (CPU)
- Random Access Memory (RAM)
- Secondary Storage (disk drive)
- Peripherals (networking, input devices, audio and video support, etc.)

Depending upon the type and/or size of the computer, the components of a computer may be located on one or more circuit boards (as depicted above), an integrated circuit, or a single chip. Now let's dig a little deeper and examine each of these components in more detail.

Central Processing Unit

The *brain* of a computer is its Central Processing Unit (CPU); it executes the instructions of computer programs to perform the operations it supports. These instructions are typically arithmetic or logic operations (e.g., add or subtract two numbers), control flow operations (go directly to a specific instruction, potentially skipping over others), or data handling operations (move data to/from memory). A CPU is itself composed of several components – an Arithmetic Logic Unit (ALU), a control unit (CU), and CPU memory.

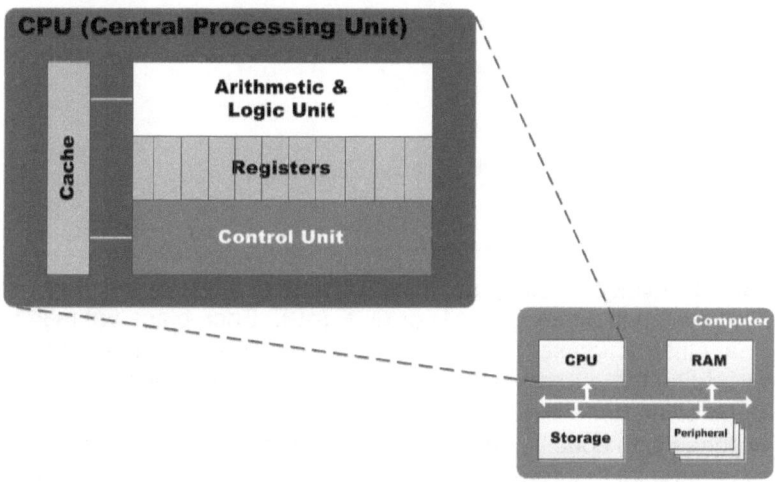

Figure 9. CPU Internals

The ALU contains circuitry to execute arithmetic and logical operations. Its arithmetic operations are addition, subtraction, multiplication, and division. Its logical operations can compare numbers, letters, or special characters; the computer can then take action based on the result of the comparison. The internal CPU memory consists of *registers* and one or more *caches*. The registers are small memory units on the CPU, each of which is capable of holding data or a machine instruction. A cache is a small memory unit, also located on the CPU, that stores copies of data from the most frequently used *RAM* memory locations. The CPU is designed such that it looks for data and instructions first in its cache(s) before searching RAM. The CU, as the name implies, controls the operation of the CPU itself. It takes the program instructions stored in memory and then decodes and executes them, using the ALU as necessary. Hence the CU controls the flow of data through the CPU and also coordinates activities within it.

Every CPU has a machine code *instruction set* which corresponds to the instructions it supports. Almost all computers are *binary machines*, meaning that each machine code instruction is a binary number. For those of you not familiar with the binary numeral system, it represents numeric values using only two symbols: 0 and 1. As with decimal numbers, when the symbols for the first digit are used, the next-higher digit (to the left) is incremented, and counting starts over at zero. The following table shows the corresponding binary values for decimal numbers 0 - 10.

Numeric Value	0	1	2	3	4	5	6	7	8	9	10
Binary Number	0	1	10	11	100	101	110	111	1000	1001	1010

Table 2. Decimal - Binary Number Relationship

You can think of a computer's instructions as a set of switches; each switch is either ON (=1) or OFF (=0). Each place value in a binary instruction set represents a switch. Hence an instruction for adding the numeric values stored in two CPU registers might be machine code like 00000001 11000001, this indicates 16 switches with specific ON/OFF values. A machine instruction contains a lot of information; it can specify the type of operation to perform (addition, subtraction, etc.), the register(s) or memory used, data, etc. A CPU is built to sequentially fetch instructions from memory and execute them, exactly as they are written.

Executing an Instruction
Before an instruction can be executed, program instructions and data must be placed into memory from an input device or a secondary storage device. The following figure depicts the steps a CPU performs to execute each instruction.

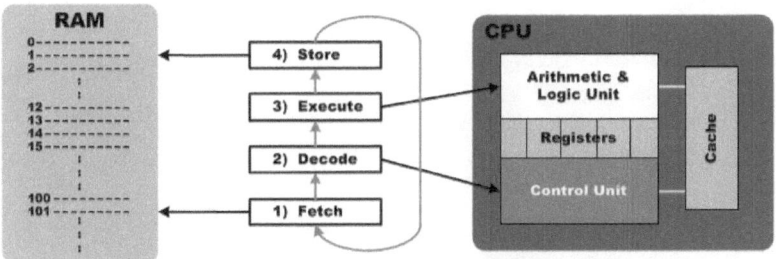

Figure 10. CPU Instruction Execution

1. The CU fetches (gets) the instruction from memory.
2. The CU decodes the instruction (decides what it means) and directs that the necessary data be moved from memory to the arithmetic/logic unit.
3. The ALU executes the arithmetic or logical instruction; that is, the ALU is given control and performs the actual operation(s) on the data.
4. The ALU stores the result of this operation in memory or in a register.

The CU eventually directs memory to release the result to an output device or a secondary storage device.

Random Access Memory

RAM, also known as the computer's *main memory*, is a form of data storage that holds both a program's instructions and data for processing. Main memory consists of a sequence of numbered locations, and the sequence number of a data location is called its memory *address*. An address provides a means of retrieving a particular piece of data from among the huge amount of data stored in memory.

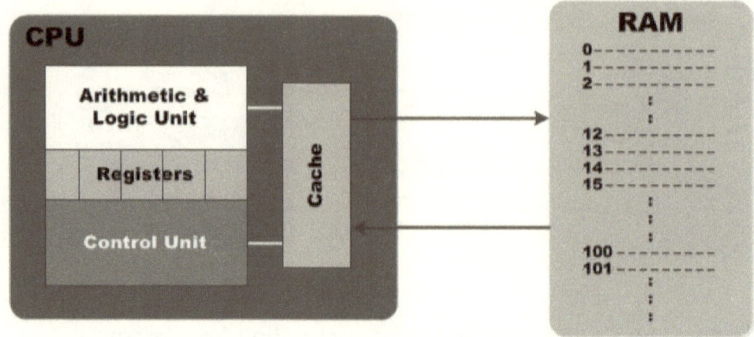

Figure 11. CPU - RAM Interaction

RAM is *volatile* memory. This means that the contents of RAM memory are lost if the computer is powered off. As the name states, it supports random access, meaning that its data elements can be accessed in any order (i.e. from any address) in relatively constant time. RAM is directly accessible by the CPU, and thus provides very fast access (although not as fast as that provided by registers and caches). Also, RAM memory has much more capacity than CPU registers or caches; modern home computers can have gigabytes of main memory, whereas cache memory capacity is in the megabytes.

In desktop and laptop computers, the amount of RAM memory is configurable. The computer has one or more memory slots on its motherboard/circuit, thus enabling you to install a variable amount of memory.

Using Cache and RAM

We mentioned earlier that RAM has very fast access, but not as fast as that of cache memory. During the course of execution of a program, some instructions (and even data) tend to be used more frequently than others. The architecture for cache memory and RAM is designed to take advantage of this phenomenon to minimize the time required to access data, thus maximizing computer performance. The following diagram depicts this interaction.

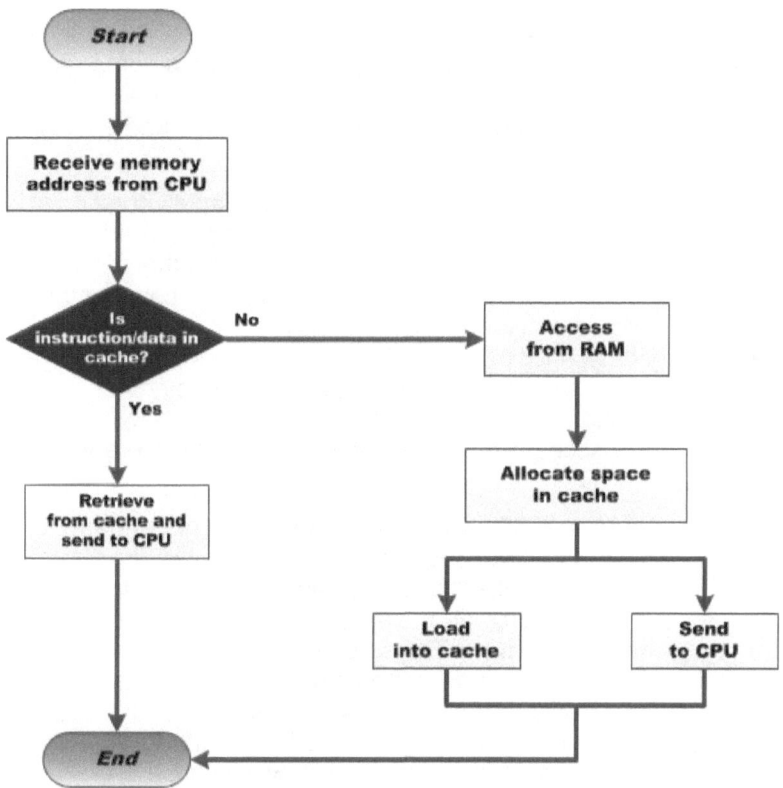

Figure 12. Cache-RAM Access Strategy

1. CPU attempts to retrieve data/instruction from cache.
2. If found, the CPU retrieves it and proceeds with instruction processing.
3. If not found, the CPU attempts to retrieve the data/instruction from RAM.
4. If found, the CPU stores the data/instruction in RAM (for future access) and proceeds with instruction processing.

CPUs have a variety of circuitry to maximize the number of cache hits and hence improve overall execution performance. Modern CPUs have a hit rate of at least 80%, meaning that at least 80% of the time the CPU isn't accessing the RAM memory directly, but the memory cache instead.

Disk Drives

Disk drives are used to permanently store data on a computer. There are several types of disk drives commonly in use today: hard disk drives (HDDs), solid-state drives (SSDs), and optical disk drives (ODDs).

An HDD consists of one or more magnetized, rapidly rotating disks on which are recorded data. Data is written to/read from a disk by means of read-write heads that can detect the magnetization of the drive and convert this information into the corresponding data. Hard disk drives have for many years been the primary device for permanent data storage. Modern HDDs are inexpensive and have very high capacity; terabytes of information can be stored on them. However, they have relatively slow access times (compared to the other storage types).

A solid-state drive (SSD) is a relatively new type of permanent data storage device that uses non-volatile electronic circuits to store data; they retain their data even when the computer is powered off. SSDs provide the same type of access as that of a traditional hard disk drive. They are generally much faster than HDDs, as they have no moving parts and relatively constant access times. SSDs also have the same interface as HDDs, thereby making it easy to substitute one for a comparable HDD. However, the storage capacity of a SSD, while higher than RAM, is lower than that of HDDs. SDDs are also generally much more expensive than HDDs.

An optical disk drive (ODD) is a disk drive that uses laser light or electromagnetic waves for reading or writing data to/from optical disks. Unlike HDDs that use magnetic disks to store data, an optical disk is coated with a special material that enables the encoding of indentations on the disk to represent data. Optical disks support three recording types: read-only (e.g. CD and CD-ROM), recordable (write-once, e.g. CD-R), and re-recordable (rewritable, e.g. CD-RW). There are multiple formats of optical disks, including CD, DVD, and Blu-ray. Access times are slower with ODDs

The following chart shows the relationships between the various storage types, speed, capacity, cost, and volatility.

Storage	Speed	Capacity	Relative Cost	Volatile?
Register	Fastest	Lowest	Highest	Yes
Cache	Extremely Fast	Low	High	Yes
RAM	Very Fast	Moderate	Moderate/High	Yes
Solid State Drive	Fast	Moderate/High	Moderate	No
Hard Disk Drive	Moderate	Very High	Very Low	No
Optical Disk Drive	Slow	Moderate (per disk)	Low (per disk)	No

Table 3. Computer Memory Characteristics

So, what type of storage should you select for your computer, and how much? Many people want the fastest, greatest amount of memory they can get for the least amount of money. Well, given the table above, it should be pretty obvious that there are tradeoffs involved here - not only is the fastest memory more expensive, it also has lower capacity. Hence it is helpful to have an understanding of how you plan on using your computer to determine what type and amount of memory to get. Let's start by figuring out the type of memory we need.

Computers primarily use RAM for executing programs, hence as both the programs we run and their memory requirements increase, the more RAM you want to have. For example, if you are primarily using your computer for browsing the web, checking email, and doing some word processing, then your RAM requirements are relatively minimal. As your needs grow, for example maybe you need to run business applications, play the latest video games, etc., your RAM requirements are moderate. Finally if you use graphics-intensive programs, enjoy complex multimedia gaming, maybe even run an online business, then your RAM requirements are very significant. It all really depends on how you plan on using your computer. My general recommendation is to get as much RAM memory as you can afford (and then a little more on top of that), because over time the programs you run always seem to need more RAM. Now let's look at the amount of storage we need.

Non-volatile storage needs are, as expected, a function of how much data you need to store permanently. As you store more and larger files/data/programs, your storage requirements grow accordingly. These days it is not uncommon for people to have desktop computers with over a terabyte of storage, particularly if they are storing multimedia files (movies, music, etc.). Here again you have a couple of things to consider, but in this case the recommendations are a function of the type of computer you are using. As it is difficult to add storage to a device or a laptop, I recommend configuring these computers with as much storage as you can afford. However, for a desktop computer there is less of a need to max out the storage on purchase, as you generally have much more flexibility for adding storage later as your needs change/grow.

Virtual Memory

As you are probably aware of by now, most computers have a lot more disk storage than RAM memory. Remembering our earlier discussion on a computer CPU, programs must be loaded into RAM to execute. RAM memory is volatile; hence the programs (both instructions and data) stored there are lost when the computer is powered off or reset. If a program is not in RAM, it must be retrieved from disk before being run. Since disk access is much slower than RAM access overall system performance suffers; as a user what you experience is a wait while the computer transfers a program into RAM for execution. The takeaway is this – the amount of RAM a computer has directly impacts its performance. So, given that we have a limited amount of RAM, how do we minimize the amount of time it takes to load programs into RAM and also maximize the amount of programs the computer can switch between? If you answered *virtual memory,* congratulations, you're right! Virtual memory is a memory management technique that addresses the problem of finite computing resources, specifically the limited amount of RAM available to execute a program. It makes all of a computer's data storage (its RAM and disk drives) behave like RAM, thereby reducing the frequency of data transfers from disk. This improves performance and also simplifies how programs manage memory. All modern computers (including desktop and laptop computers) and many devices include a virtual memory system.

Virtual Memory in Action

The location of data in memory is specified by its *memory address*. Virtual memory works by providing a memory range (also known as a *virtual address space*) for each program. This virtual address space is often larger than the actual available

RAM and is divided into sections, referred to as *pages*. A *page table* is used to map these virtual addresses to actual RAM memory addresses. Typically this translation of virtual addresses to physical addresses is performed by a computer component called a *memory management unit*. So when a computer executes program code and/or accesses data, it uses the program's corresponding virtual memory addresses and page table to locate it in RAM. If not found, it retrieves the associated program code/data from disk, stores it in RAM for execution, and updates the virtual memory and page tables appropriately.

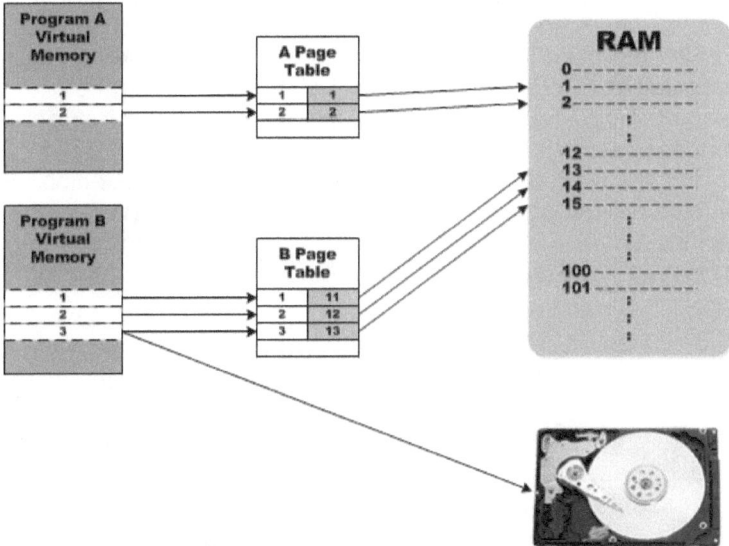

Figure 13. Virtual Memory Architecture

As an example, let's say that **Program A** begins execution. The program points to virtual memory addresses. The computer's memory management unit uses a page table to retrieve the program code/data at the corresponding RAM physical address (RAM address block 1). Now **Program B** resumes execution and requires code/data at virtual memory address block 3. The memory management unit cannot find this data in RAM, so it must be loaded from storage and stored in RAM so that the program can continue execution. The corresponding page table is also updated. The next time **Program B** needs to access code/data in address block 3, it does this from RAM. And there you have it, that's virtual memory in action!

Peripherals

A peripheral is a device connected to a computer that expands its capabilities. Peripherals provide a variety of functionality, including I/O, networking, memory, communication, audio and video support, etc. They usually communicate with the other computer components by means of communication buses and ports. Some common peripheral devices include keyboards, pointing devices (mouse, touch pad, etc.), monitors, printers, disk drives (flash drives, HDDs, ODDs), scanners, and audio equipment.

Communication buses are typically designed to connect multiple devices. There are multiple varieties of communication buses, and they are used for different purposes. A (main) memory bus connects the CPU to system memory (RAM) and potentially cache memory. Serial ATA (SATA) is a communication bus for connecting storage devices such as hard disk drives. PCI Express (PCIe) is an expansion bus used for communication with external peripherals such as Ethernet, wireless (WiFi), and graphics cards. Universal Serial Bus (USB) standardizes the connection of various types of peripherals to a communication bus.

A port is a specialized outlet that serves as an interface between the computer and peripheral devices; a peripheral is connected to the computer at a port outlet via its corresponding plug. Some common ports on computers include the USB port, Ethernet port (used for network cable connections), DVI port (commonly used for computer monitors), parallel port (commonly used for printers), and TRS connectors (used for audio).

A connector is a specialized outlet, like a port, which serves as an interface between the computer and peripheral devices. Unlike a port, a connector may also be internal, i.e. directly on the computer motherboard or circuit. Some common connectors include the SATA connector (for HDDs).

Now that we have reviewed all of the main components of a computer along with some common peripherals we'll end this section with a look at the following detailed block diagram.

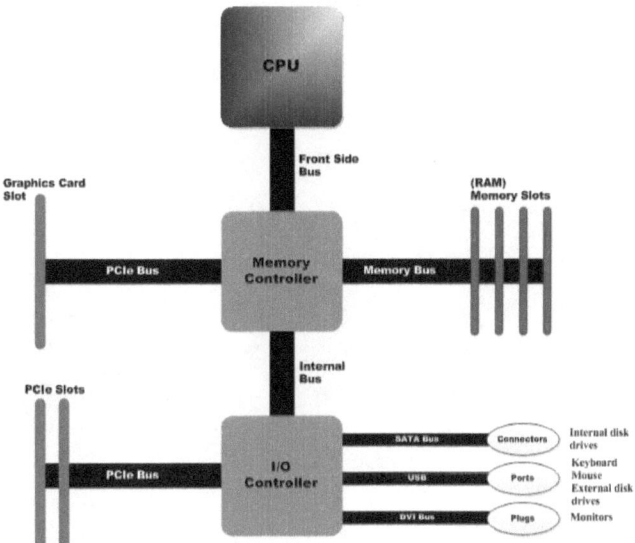

Figure 14. Computer Detailed Diagram

It depicts a computer that contains a CPU, a memory controller that communicates with the CPU via a front-side bus, several communication buses for RAM memory and a graphics card, and an internal bus for communication with an I/O controller that supports PCI cards, disk drives, I/O devices (keyboard, mouse), and monitors.

Summary

This chapter provided you with an overview of the inner workings of a computer. You now have a basic understanding of its main components and how they work together to run programs. With this background, you should feel more comfortable discussing computers the next time you're out shopping for a PC or device. In the meantime, why not spend a moment to reflect on what we've covered so far. In the next chapter we'll return to programming as we learn about social networking and how to write Facebook applications.

Chapter 7
Social Networking

Social network websites are all about connections. The connections can be with people, places, and businesses, in fact just about anything these days. There are numerous social network sites supporting all kinds of interests and practices, and nowadays they touch nearly every facet of our lives. These sites make it easier to share news and other information, and have pretty much transformed how people interact in modern society. So you may be saying, "Yeah, I use Facebook, Twitter, LinkedIn, YouTube, and other sites, but what does this have to do with programming?" Well, in this chapter you're going find out how to extend social network websites by learning how to write your own programs for them. Believe it or not, this is something that you can do yourself and it can enhance your experience with these websites, so let's try it out!

Social Network Applications

Many social network websites include programming tools and APIs to facilitate application development. Several programming options are commonly supported:

- Host integration
  This option enables you to create an external web application that integrates directly with a social network website.

- Public APIs
  Many social network websites provide Application
  Programming Interfaces (APIs) that enable you to write
  programs or web applications to access information from
  its site over a standard protocol (e.g. over the Internet).

Host Integration

Some social networks enable you to build a web application that
is displayed within its own (social network) website, e.g.
Facebook. As the number of social media users is now over one
billion and continues to climb, this integration approach can
greatly extend the online presence of an entity, through the
power of social networking. For example, A Facebook user can
download an app (i.e. a web application) that you built and made
available through the host integration option; when the user
selects this app this website is displayed right on Facebook.com.
The user is then able to view all of the website content,
recommend it to friends, etc. Also, as the website runs within
Facebook.com, it has access to user information; this information
can be used to enhance the user experience.

Public APIs

An API specifies an interface for communication between
software components. It defines the messages that can be sent,
the data that can be transferred, etc. Many social network
websites provide public APIs that are implemented over a
standard communications protocol, specifically HTTP. This
enables you to write programs that use a public API to interact
with these websites. For example, one set of Twitter APIs
enables you to view and segment the timeline on which all real-
time tweets arrive. The following API call (actually an HTTP
request)

```
http://api.twitter.com/1/statuses/public_timeline.xml
```

returns the 20 most recent public tweets from users with a
custom profile picture. Public APIs make it easy to write
programs that communicate with social network websites.

Security

Social network sites control access to confidential information.
Hence to use social network apps (i.e. host integration) or APIs
users may need to be logged-in (i.e. *authenticated*) and may also
require the appropriate permissions. Together the requirement
for authentication and the appropriate permissions is considered

access control. Social network sites provide a variety of mechanisms to support access control using a supported programming mechanism.

Facebook Application Programming

Now that we have reviewed some of the common mechanisms used for programming social network websites, we can explore Facebook application programming. The Facebook platform provides extensive infrastructure for application development and integration. This includes tools and services for developing websites hosted on Facebook.com, APIs available for use by external applications, and SDKs for mobile app integration. This section will prepare you for developing Facebook apps, starting with an overview of the Facebook platform components and concluding with a discussion of application development options.

Facebook Platform

The Facebook platform provides a set of APIs and tools, which enable you to develop programs that integrate with Facebook.com. Some of its principle components are the Graph API, Facebook Markup Language for websites (XFBML), Authentication APIs, social plug-ins, the Open Graph protocol, and Facebook Connect. In the following paragraphs we'll take a detailed look at these components to understand how they can be used to build Facebook apps.

Graph API

Many social network sites utilize *social graphs* to establish and maintain connections between its users. A social graph depicts personal relations; the relations can be biological, to friends, common interests (e.g. likes), etc. The Facebook Platform provides a set of APIs and tools that enable third-party developers to integrate with the Facebook social graph, whether through applications on Facebook or external websites and devices. The Facebook Graph API allows you to access data about any user on Facebook in an organized form through a web browser. Data is requested by typing into the browser the URL `https://graph.facebook.com/`*`name_ID`*`/`*`item`*, where *`name_ID`* is the Facebook username or ID for the user, and *`item`* is the specific data item from the user's graph that you want to retrieve. The data is returned as a **JSON**-formatted list – JSON stands for JavaScript Object Notation, a standard format for textual data. For example, the URL

```
https://graph.facebook.com/zuck
```

retrieves a graph of basic information for the Facebook user with a username of `zuck`.

The graph has a set of Publically Accessible Information (PAI) that can be retrieved without user authentication. The PAI data set consists of a user's

- Name
- Profile picture URL
- Gender
- Any networks the user belongs to
- User ID
- Locale
- Friends (along with the same information as the user's friends)
- Any information the user sets to "Everyone" access in his/her privacy settings.

An example set of PAI data (in JSON format) is

```
{
  "id": "4",
  "name": "Mark Zuckerberg",
  "first_name": "Mark",
  "last_name": "Zuckerberg",
  "link": "http://www.facebook.com/zuck",
  "username": "zuck",
  "gender": "male",
  "locale": "en_US"
}
```

Facebook provides SDKs in several programming languages that make it simple to use the graph API to access data. For example, the Facebook JavaScript SDK can be used on a web page to access a graph object with the following code

```
FB.api('/me', function(response)
{
  alert(response.name);

});
```

This code uses `FB.api`; a graph API provided with the JavaScript SDK, to retrieve the PAI of the currently logged-in user and then display his/her name in an alert box. In order to login a user and/or access protected user graph API data the user has to provide permission; this is where the authentication APIs are used.

Authentication APIs

Facebook provides a couple of methods to authorize applications to access its platform. The simple mechanism uses JavaScript to authenticate the user and assign permissions to access user data. The recommended, general-purpose approach is to develop your applications with Open Authorization (OAuth) 2.0. OAuth allows Facebook users to share their private resources with an external site without having to provide their credentials (i.e. a Facebook username/password pair), instead supplying *tokens*. Each token grants access to a specific site for specific resources for a defined duration.

OAuth works by sending users through a Facebook-hosted login process, in which they authorize your application to access specific bits of information about them. In return, Facebook returns a token back to your application for further requests on the Facebook Platform. The sequence of events is as follows:

1. User attempts to access Facebook-provided information (via the Facebook Graph API) from an external website.
2. Website redirects user to the Facebook login page.
3. User submits Facebook login information (username and password).
4. If login succeeds, external website is returned a token that it uses to retrieve the Facebook-provided information requested in Step 1.

The OAuth API provides a powerful and easy-to-use mechanism for integrating authentication and authorization into Facebook apps.

XFBML

The Facebook Markup Language for Web sites (XFBML) is a simple markup language created to facilitate rapid development of Facebook-enabled web sites. XFBML tags can be used within inline frames (iFrames) on Facebook.com, as well as on external web sites. The example below shows the code for initializing a Facebook application using XFBML and some simple JavaScript; this code would nominally be placed right below the `<body>` tag of a web page.

```
<div id=" fb-root"></div>
<script
  src="http://connect.facebook.net/en_US/all.js">
</script>
<script>
  FB.init({appId: 'yourappidgoeshere', status:
    true, cookie: true, xfbml: true});
</script>
```

This code identifies your application and initializes the Facebook object in JavaScript so that you can make more calls to Facebook on the page. (Be sure to replace *yourappid-goeshere* with the application ID you received during your application setup in the preceding section!)

Social Plugins

Social plugins provide an easy way to build a Facebook-integrated website. A plugin is custom HTML content which you can copy and paste into web pages on your own websites. Your web pages are then updated with this content that interacts directly with Facebook from your website. There are many social plugins available and more are being created; those available for use now include

- Like Button
- Login Button
- Comments
- Facepile
- Live Stream

The list of Facebook plugins currently available is provided at http://developers.facebook.com/plugins. You should visit this site to find out more information on existing plugins, along with new ones as they become available.

Open Graph Protocol

The Open Graph Protocol (OGP) enables developers to integrate web pages into the Facebook social graph. It consists of a series of *meta tags* (HTML elements that provide descriptive information about a web page), which identify what a specific website or URL is about. They enable a website to add metadata into its web pages that can declare the identity or function of the site and can specify the way the site owner would like the site to be indexed by Facebook. In this manner, OGP can be used to tailor how a Facebook user searches for a website. You add an OGP tag to a website's meta tags, using the format `<meta property="`**`tag name`**`" content="`**`tag content`**`">`. Some common OGP tags include

- `og:title` – The title you want to show up in the user's stream when he or she clicks the Like button for your page.
- `og:type` – The "type" of an object, for example "video.movie". For the item being liked, this is where it will be placed in a user's Likes and Interests section on the user's Info tab for his or her profile.
- `og:image` – An image URL which should represent an object within the Facebook graph.
- `og:url` – The full URL of the object that will be used as its permanent ID in the graph.

A complete list of the available OGP tags is provided at https://developers.facebook.com/docs/opengraphprotocol/.

Facebook Connect

Facebook Connect is a set of APIs that enable Facebook members to login to external websites and applications using their Facebook identity. It has four main features

- Trusted Authentication – Users can connect their Facebook account with any partner website/application using a trusted authentication method, with total control of the permissions granted.
- Real Identity – On partner websites/application, users can represent themselves with their real names and identities.
- Friends Access – Users will be able to take their friends with them, enabling developers to add social content to their partner websites/applications.
- Dynamic Privacy – Privacy settings and controls are included, ensuring that these are up to date and consistent.

Application Development Options

Facebook provides several options for application development. These enable you to integrate Facebook features into an existing website via a public API, integrate a web application within the Facebook platform, or integrate Facebook features into a mobile app.

The **website** option integrates Facebook features into your own web application. The Facebook platform APIs makes it possible to retrieve almost any type of data about users and their friends and apply it to your own web site's content.

A **hosted** Facebook application is a web application integrated with the Facebook platform. These apps are hosted externally but accessed from Facebook.com; they can be built with any language or tool that supports web programming, such as HTML, JavaScript, or PHP.

A **mobile** Facebook app enables you to integrate Facebook features into a mobile app. Facebook provides software development kits (SDKs) for iOS and Android devices to do this.

Creating a Simple Facebook App

Now that you have a good overview of several key elements of the Facebook platform, you're ready to learn how to build your own Facebook app! Application development for the Facebook platform continues to evolve a rapid pace, so much so that it makes little sense to provide detailed step-by-step instructions. Instead here you'll get an overview of the steps involved to integrate a web application on Facebook.com, along with an example that shows how you can customize a web application to use the features provided by the platform. Overall, the steps for developing a Facebook App (i.e., integrating a web application on Facebook) are:

1. Create a new app on Facebook.
2. Build a web application using your desired web technologies (HTML, JavaScript, CSS, PHP, etc.) and host this web application on a web-hosting provider.
3. Configure your Facebook app settings so that the web application you developed in Step 2 is integrated on Facebook.com.

Now let's go over these steps in more detail to understand the actions required.

Create a Facebook App (Step 1)

The first step is to create a Facebook account if you don't already have one. Next go to the Facebook Developers site (https://developers.facebook.com/); it provides plenty of essential documentation for developers and application owners. Specifically, you should review the documentation on building a

Facebook app (including the tutorial if present). When you are ready you can begin the process of setting up your new Facebook App, per the instructions documented at the Facebook Developers site; note that you may be required to supply inputs (App Name, etc.) on one or more screens.

Once you have finished the initial setup steps for your new Facebook app, you can now build and host your web application.

Build and Host the Web Application (Step 2)

As the focus of this exercise is to understand the steps to build a Facebook app, we have provided an example web application for your use. This web app demonstrates the type of information at your disposal for integration with the Facebook platform. It is a simple web page (*index.html*) that uses HTML, CSS, JavaScript, and Facebook APIs to display a greeting and the user's name. The code is shown below; first look it over and then we'll talk about it.

```
<!DOCTYPE html>
<html>
  <body>
    <div id="fb-root"></div>
    <script src="http://connect.facebook.net/en_US/all.js" charset="utf-8">
    </script>
    <script>
      FB.init(
      {
        appId: '319314101490582',
        status: true,
        cookie: true,
        xfbml: true
      });
      FB.getLoginStatus(function(response)
      {
        if (response.status === 'connected')
        {
          FB.api('/me', function(graph)
          {
            document.getElementById("name").innerHTML = graph.name;
            document.getElementById("username").innerHTML = graph.username;
          });
        }
        else
        {
          FB.login(function(loginRes)
          {
            if (loginRes.authResponse)
            {
              FB.api('/me', function(graph)
              {
                document.getElementById("name").innerHTML = graph.name;
                document.getElementById("username").innerHTML = graph.username;
              });
            }
            else
            {
              document.getElementById("name").innerHTML = "User";
              document.getElementById("username").innerHTML =
                "Unknown (not logged in)";
            }
          });
        }
      });
    </script>

    <div style="font-size: xx-large;">
      Hello,
      <div id="name" style="display: inline"></div>
    </div>
    <div style="font-size: x-large;">
      Your Facebook username is
      <div id="username" style="display: inline;"></div>
    </div>
  </body>
</html>
```

Figure 15. Facebook Web Application

This web page uses the Facebook JavaScript SDK to authenticate the user to use this app and the Graph API for retrieving the users PAI. It then displays the user's name and username on the page. Starting at the top of the document the code

```
<div id="fb-root"></div>
```

is placed after the opening <body> tag in the web page. This is required in order for the JavaScript SDK to load properly. Next the JavaScript SDK libraries are imported with the tag

```
<script
  src="http://connect.facebook.net/en_US/all.js"
  charset="utf-8">
```

The `FB.init` API initializes the SDK with the appropriate
settings. The remainder of the JavaScript code is within the
`FB.getLoginStatus` API; it authenticates the user for the app,
and once authenticated the Graph API is used to retrieve PAI
data. Specifically the statement

```
FB.api('/me', function(graph)
```

retrieves this data for the currently authenticated user. The
HTML on the page

```
<div style="font-size: xx-large;">
  Hello,
  <div id="name" style="display: inline"></div>
</div>
<div style="font-size: x-large;">
  Your Facebook username is
  <div id="username"
    style="display: inline;"></div>
</div>
```

Displays the data retrieved using the SDK and the Graph API on
the page.

Once you finish developing your web application, you have to
host it on a web server so that it can be accessed over the web.
The basic steps for doing this are

1. Selecting a hosting provider to serve up your web
    pages,
2. Registering a domain,
3. Configuring your account at the hosting provider with
    your new domain,
4. Storing your web pages at the hosting provider, and
5. Configuring your web pages at the hosting provider so
    that they will be served from your new domain.

There are numerous web-hosting providers to select from and
many of them will perform all of the above services. You can
find a list of available providers by performing a search using
your search engine of choice, under the category of "web hosting
providers".

Configure the Facebook App Basic Settings (Step 3)
Now navigate back to the Facebook Developers Apps site (https://developers.facebook.com/apps) and complete the configuration of the Facebook App you created in Step 1. Specifically, your Facebook App must be integrated with (i.e. point to) the web application you built in Step 2 so that it can be displayed on Facebook. Make sure to review the documentation at the Facebook Developers site for instructions on how to do this; at the time of this writing the minimum set of parameters you must configure are the **Canvas URL** and **Secure Canvas URL**. The Canvas URL is the URL for the web application you created and hosted previously. Provide an appropriate Secure Canvas URL; if you don't have one you can enter the same URL as supplied for the Canvas URL, substituting `https` for `http`.

Test Your App
Now let's test your new app; from your browser go to `http://apps.facebook.com/`**app_name,** where **app_name** is the name of your app as provided in Step 1. If all has gone well, you should now be able to view your app on Facebook!

Summary
Congratulations, you've made it this far, great job! You now have a good start on social networks and how to develop programs that work with this technology. Keep in mind that social network websites continue to grow and evolve, so it's always a good idea to check the resources available online for each site that you want to program for. With the tools you have at your disposal, you're now on your way to becoming proficient at programming for the social web!

Chapter **8**
The Programmer's Toolkit

No matter what programming language you choose, the tools you use for software development will have a major impact on the ease and efficiency with which you develop programs. In this chapter we'll look at some of the most common items in the programmer's toolkit, and provide you with a couple of programming examples that will allow you to get experience using these tools.

Program Development Tools

Having the right tools and knowing how to use them can make all the difference, no matter what the task. For computer programming several essential tools are a *source code editor*, a *build tool*, and a *debugger*. These tools are usually packaged together in an application called an Integrated Development Environment (IDE). IDEs are designed to include every tool and resource a programmer would need to develop almost any type of application. There are quite a few IDEs available at this time; common ones include Apple's Xcode and Microsoft's Visual Studio. Features that distinguish IDEs are things like the programming language(s) they support and the features they provide to aid application development. As many IDEs support several programming languages, the one you choose often depends on factors like its feature set and your experience/ease with using it. Later on in this chapter you'll have the opportunity to use several different IDEs to write a simple program.

Source Code Editor

A source code editor is a text-editing program designed specifically for writing computer programs. These tools differ from plain text editors like Microsoft Notepad in that they include features designed to simplify editing code and also increase programmer efficiency. For example, many source code editors include capabilities for checking your source code and notifying you of any typing errors, performing auto-completion while you type, and formatting your code to make it easier to read. Source code editors also typically provide a convenient way to run a build automation tool or debugger.

As many programs have graphical user interfaces (GUIs), it is also common to find a GUI designer that simplifies the creation of GUIs. A GUI designer can be considered as a special type of editor that enables the programmer to create a GUI in a more intuitive manner, by manually arranging GUI elements on the screen as required.

Build Automation Tools

As a programmer you use build automation tools to turn the program that you have written into an application that can be run on a computer. These tools automate the process of performing a variety of tasks, including

- Compiling source code into machine code.
- Testing the source code and/or machine code and reporting any errors found.
- Packaging machine code so that it can be executed by a target computer/device.
- Deploying executable machine code onto the target computer/device.

Some IDEs include additional build automation functionality such as reporting, creation of program documentation, and tools to manage different program versions.

Debugger

A debugger is a tool used to detect errors in an executing program. Programs commonly "crash" due to programming errors, for example the program uses an invalid instruction or sets a variable to an invalid value. Debuggers enable you to inspect an executing program to determine exactly where an error is occurring and identify the exact cause of the error.

Software Libraries

Software libraries are collections of existing software resources that can be used to develop programs. Their contents may include new and/or existing software modules, specifications, data, documentation, and other resources. Software libraries differ from programs in that they typically cannot be executed as is, but rather are used to implement an executable program. It is common to find software libraries that perform

- Data structure manipulation
- Data processing for various data formats
- Implementation of computer security mechanisms
- Enabling program communication with other systems
- Mathematical processing
- User interface development support
- Multimedia support
- Graphics and image manipulation

Good software libraries are vital for efficient application development; the more useful the functionality implemented by your software libraries the less code you have to write.

Many programming languages come with one or more standard (i.e. *core*) libraries.

Software Platform

A software platform is the combination of a programming language along with its associated software libraries. The software platform and corresponding program development tools with are often a key factor in the success or failure of a software development project.

Creating a Project with Xcode

Now that you have a basic understanding of IDEs and how they are used to write programs, let's use the Apple Xcode IDE to create an Objective-C program. Xcode 4, the current release, is a complete toolset for building Mac OS X and iOS applications. It includes a source code editor, a graphical user interface editor, a compiler with full support for Objective-C (along with ANSI C and C++), a powerful debugger, and many other features. Xcode 4 is a free download for all members of the Apple iOS and Mac Developer Programs. If you are not a member of either program, Xcode 4 for Mac OS X Lion/Mountain Lion is also available as a free download from the Mac App Store. Xcode 4 will run on any Mac computer that has OS X Lion installed; of course the more computer resources (CPU speed, memory, disk space) you have available the better!

Once you have downloaded and installed Xcode 4, launch the program and the welcome window is displayed.

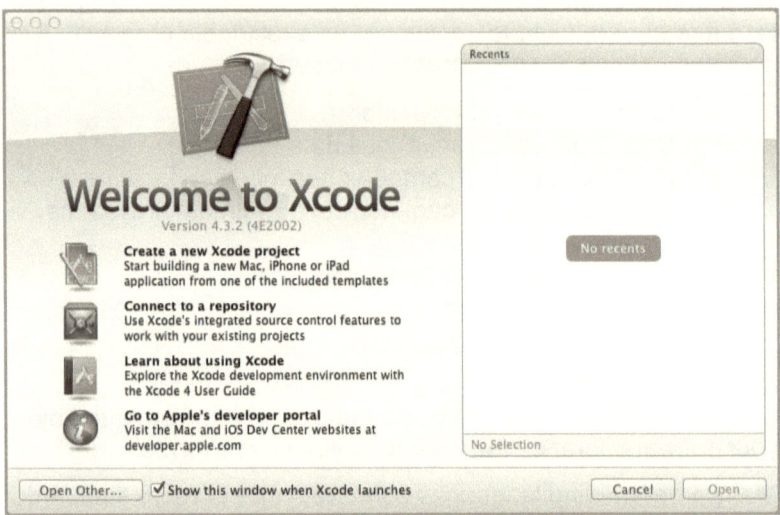

Figure 16. Xcode Welcome Window

From here a variety of options are presented, let's select the **Create a new Xcode project** option (Note that you can also create a new project by selecting **File ➜ New ➜ New Project ...** from the Xcode menu).

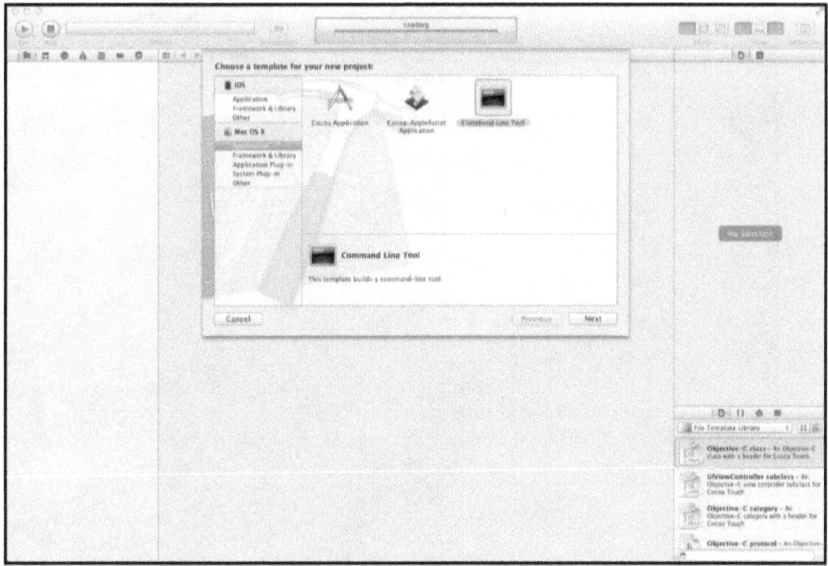

Figure 17. Xcode New Project Assistant

The Xcode IDE window is displayed; followed by the *New Project Assistant* pane on top of that. The left side of the New Project Assistant is divided into iOS and Mac OS X sections. We are going to start off by creating a command line application, so select **Application** under the Mac OS X section. In the upper-right pane you'll see several icons that represent each of the project templates that are provided as starting points for creating Mac OS X applications, select **Command Line Tool** and click **Next**. A new window will be displayed for you to input project-specific information.

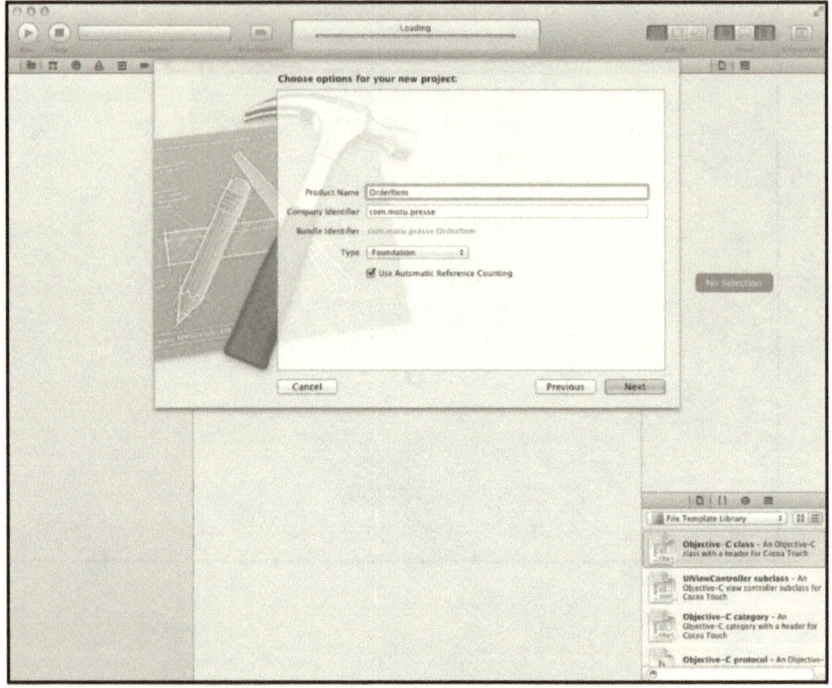

Figure 18. Xcode Project Options Window

Specify the *Product Name* for the project (for this example
OrderItem), a *Company Identifier* (this is a name used to provide
an identifier for your application, typically you input something
like your domain name in reverse order but any name will
suffice), the *Type* of application (Xcode supports various
application types, including C, C++, etc., here we select
Foundation for an Objective-C project that uses the Foundation
framework), and finally a checkbox to specify whether or not the
project will use *Automatic Reference Counting* for memory
management. After this information has been provided click
Next and a window is displayed for entering the name and
location for the project.

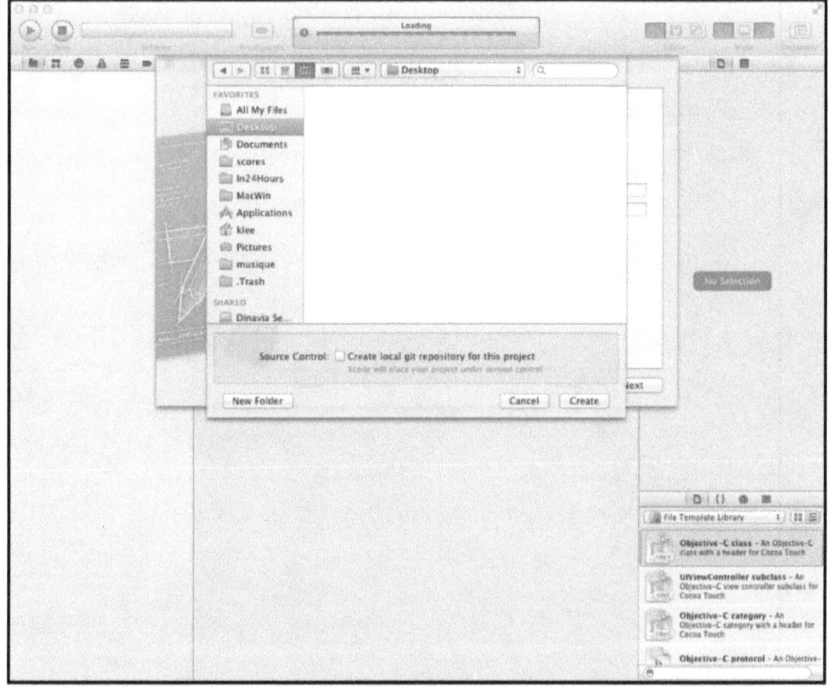

Figure 19. Xcode Project Location Window

Specify the folder where you want the project to be created (if necessary select **New Folder** and enter the name and location for the folder); do not select the **Source Control** checkbox. After this has been entered click the **Create** button and the Xcode project window opens.

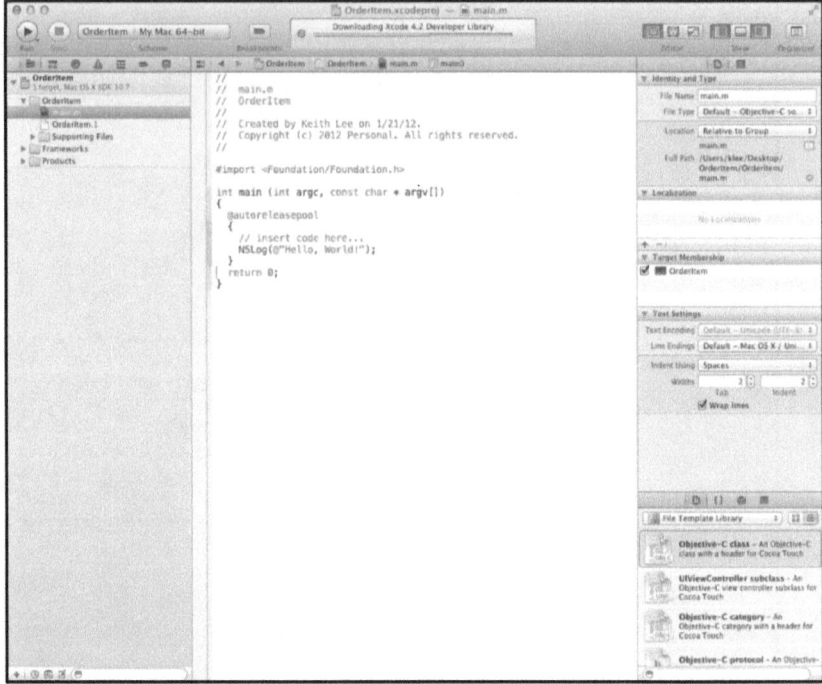

Figure 20. Xcode Project Window

You now have created an Xcode project named OrderItem. In the editor window you see a file named `main.m`; it contains the `main()` function for your program. Now earlier in this book you learned about some of the key elements of Objective-C programs, but we didn't mention the `main()` function; let's discuss this now.

The `main()` function is required for each Objective-C program and is called when the program begins execution. In the figure above you can see that Xcode creates a default main() function (in a file called `main.m`) and includes the following example code

```
NSLog(@"Hello, World!");
```

If you run this program *as-is* it will display **Hello, World!** Let's update this to have the program display a greeting along with the current date and time. Add the code shown in the figure below.

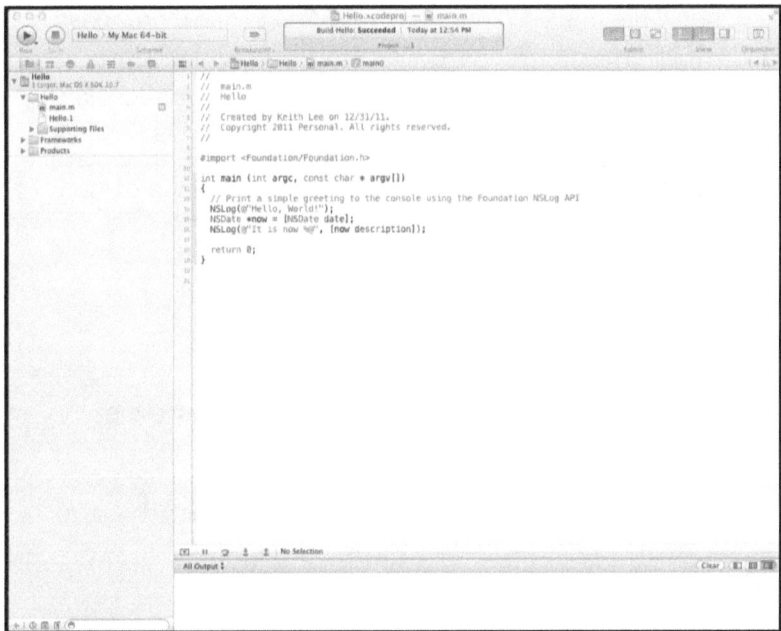

Figure 21. Hello World Program Developed Using Xcode

Now save the project (**File ➜ Save** from the Xcode menu) and run it (**Product ➜ Run** from the Xcode menu). In the output window at the bottom of the Xcode display you should see the text "Hello, World!" displayed, followed by the current date and time.

Well, that's it; you have used Xcode to create a simple Objective-C program! The Apple Xcode User Guide provides a full introduction to Xcode and its features.

Using Visual Basic

Now let's create the same program using Microsoft Visual Basic. BASIC *(Beginners All-Purpose Symbolic Instruction Code)* is one of the oldest and most commonly used programming languages. The goals for the developers of the language were to create a programming language that makes it easy for beginners to use and begin programming, without requiring an understanding of computer hardware or operating systems. Visual Basic Express is a free set of tools that can be used to create programs using BASIC. What we'll do here is create our first Visual Basic project and then write the *Hello* program in BASIC to show how easy it is to get started with both the tools and the language.

The Visual Basic Express (VBE) platform is used for developing Windows applications using the BASIC programming language. It includes an IDE, software libraries, and services. The current version of VBE (VBE 2010) is designed to run on one of the following Windows operating systems:

- Windows XP
- Windows Server 2003, 2008
- Windows Vista
- Windows 7

In addition, at a minimum your computer should have the following resources:

Requirement	Minimum	Recommended
Processor	1.6 GHz	2.2 GHz
Memory	1 GB (32-bit) 2 GB (64-bit)	3 GB
Hard Disk	1.3 GB free space	1.3 GB free space

Microsoft VBE can be downloaded from the Microsoft web site. Users must register the software to continue using it after 30 days.

To begin, download the VBE installer (**vb_web.exe**) to the folder of your choice. Once the download has completed double-click on the **vb_web.exe** file to begin installation. Follow the instructions provided by the installer to install the software (Note that it is not necessary to install the SQL package for the program we'll create here, so you can skip that if it is an option during installation). Also note that you may be prompted to restart your computer at some point during the installation; perform the restart as requested as this is a normal part of the install process.

Once the installation has been completed, start Visual Basic Express using the Windows start menu (*start* ➔ **All Programs ➔ Microsoft Visual Studio 2010 Express ➔ Microsoft Visual Basic 2010 Express**). The Visual Basic Express Start Page is displayed.

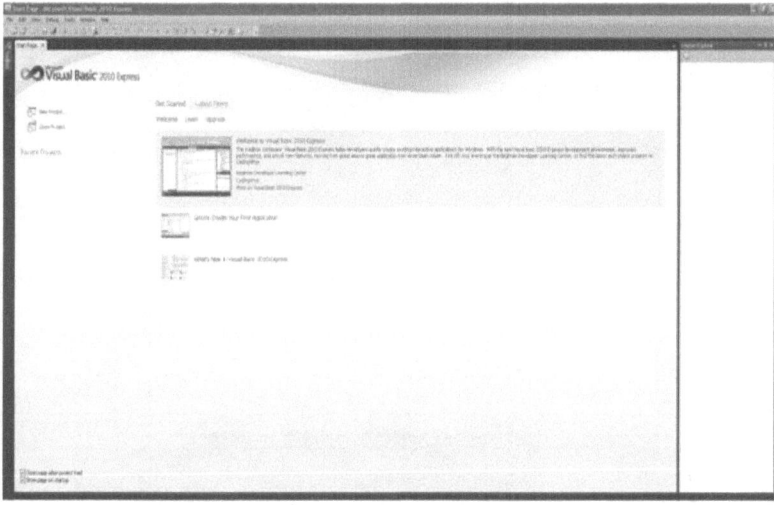

Figure 22. VBE Start Page

Now create a new VBE project by selecting the **New Project...** option on the Start Page.

Here you will see the New Project window. It includes project templates that enable you to quickly get started. Select the **Console Application** template, and at the bottom of the window name the application **Hello**.

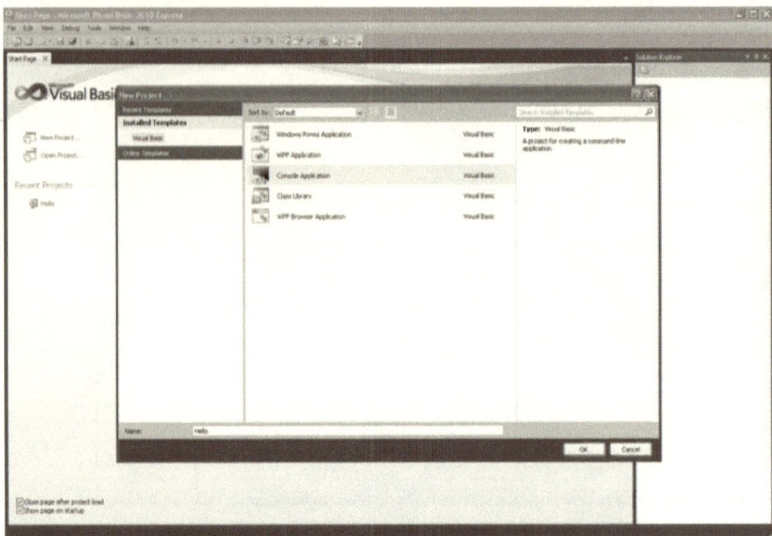

Figure 23. VBE New Project Window

The Hello project page is displayed; this project has one **Module** (named `Module1`) and one **Sub** named `Main()`.

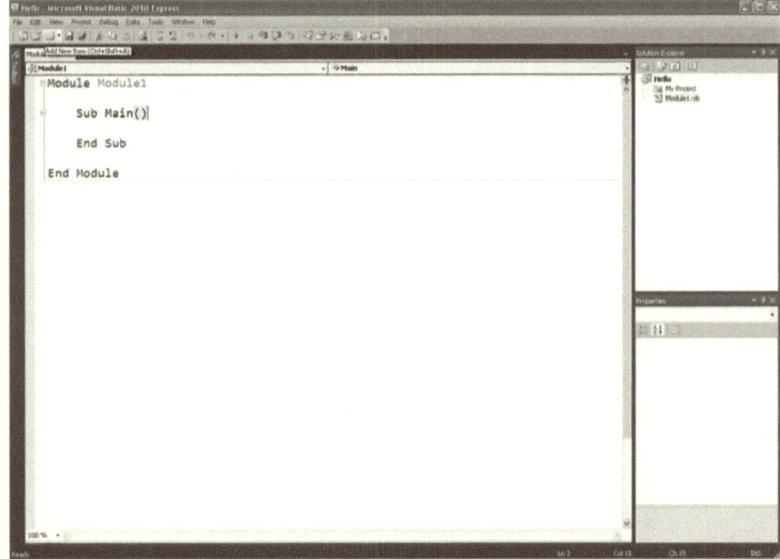

Figure 24. VBE Hello Project

A **Sub** is BASIC terminology for a *subroutine*. Subroutines are also known as functions, which you learned about in previous chapters. Note that if you compare this project to the Xcode Objective-C project we created earlier, you'll notice they look pretty similar (at least the templates do!).

Now let's add the BASIC code to display a greeting followed by the current date and time. Insert the following code between the Sub Main() and End Sub lines.

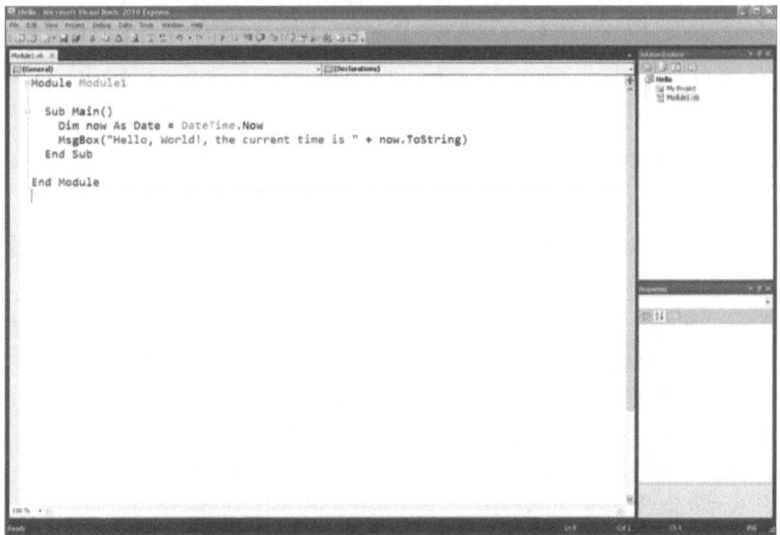

Figure 25. VBE Hello Program Code

Now compile (**Debug ➔ Build Hello**) then execute (**Debug ➔ Start Debugging**) your program; you should see a popup window that displays "Hello World!" along with the current date and time.

Programming for Everyone

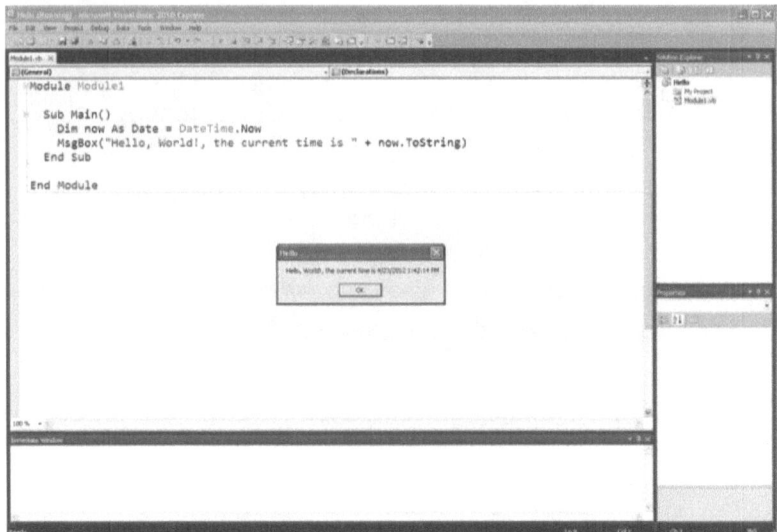

Figure 26. Hello Program Output

(Note: if you don't see the popup window, it is probably hidden; if you click on the **Hello** icon in the Windows Taskbar at the bottom of the screen the popup window will be displayed.)

And that's it; you have just created your first Visual Basic application! Microsoft has plenty of resources available online that will give you a complete introduction to Visual Basic and the programming language.

Summary

As with Xcode, an IDE along with its associated tools and software libraries make it pretty easy to get started writing programs. After doing one or both of these examples you can see why these tools are essential for programming. Now that you're pretty familiar with several programming languages and tools, along with computer hardware, perhaps it's a good time to learn how to write a mobile application. Sounds cool, let's do that in the next chapter.

Chapter **9**
Going Mobile

The growth of mobile computing shows no signs of slowing down. The many types of mobile computing devices common today include mobile phones, personal digital assistants (PDAs), tablet computers, car computers, and even wearable computers! Fueling this growth, the number of mobile apps now available for distribution is approaching one million and the number of mobile app downloads is in the tens of billions and still accelerating. So this is a great time to learn the basics of writing mobile apps, and that's the goal for this chapter. We'll start off with an overview of mobile computing and the current mobile app landscape. Next we'll look at several popular mobile app development platforms. Finally, we'll present a step-by-step guide for creating your first mobile app.

The Basics
From the ENIAC, the first general-purpose electronic computer, to today's mobile devices, computers have evolved from large and cumbersome machines that took up whole rooms to mobile devices that can be comfortably carried or even worn.

From
Mainframes

To
Devices

Fits in
Your hand

Fits in
a Room

Figure 27. The Evolution of Computers

A mobile computing device is a small, portable electronic device that typically has a touch-screen interface and/or a miniature keyboard. In addition it typically has wireless communications capabilities and is easily transportable. Mobile devices are made by numerous manufacturers and have many uses, including communications, business, entertainment, and general purpose computing. At present the mobile devices experiencing the most growth for application development are mobile phones, PDAs, and tablet computers. In fact these devices have become general platforms for running specific applications and tools, fueling the growth of the mobile app market. Mobile applications fall into many categories; some of the most common being games, news, social networking, information, entertainment (music, video), leisure, productivity, business, and communications (email, messaging, collaboration).

Device Characteristics

OK, so now that we have completed this basic introduction to the mobile device landscape and the categories of mobile apps, we can start writing applications for our phones, tablets, and other devices, right? After all, now that we've written some code and learned the basics of a few programming languages, can't we just write some more programs using the skills developed so far and load them onto our devices? Well, hold on a minute, not so fast! Mobile computing has a number of characteristics that distinguish it from traditional desktop computing; so before we start coding let's identify what these are:

- *Limited resources*
  Mobile devices have limited computing resources (compared to desktop or laptop computers) and are generally not expandable. In addition, mobile devices must rely entirely on limited battery power.

- *Constrained user interface*
  The screens and keyboards for mobile devices are small, therefore making the user interface harder to use and limiting the amount of information that can be presented to the user in a single screen.
- *Limited/intermittent network connectivity*
  Mobile network connectivity and signal reception varies according to location and does not provide continuous availability. Some technologies used to provide mobile networking include cell phone mobile networks, Wi-Fi, and Bluetooth, each of which has specific features and limitations. Data transfer rates for mobile networks are generally slower than that available with direct network connections.
- *Wireless security*
  In a wireless mobile communication environment, messages transmitted over a wireless medium are more susceptible to eavesdropping than in a wired network. Also, it is possible for any user to access the mobile communication system using a false identity.

As a programmer you need to be aware of these characteristics, as they will affect how you develop mobile applications. You'll have to write your programs to function properly and perform well despite the smaller screen size, the (at times) limited or no network connectivity, wireless networking security challenges, and resource and power constraints that require you to be able to save and close your application at a moment's notice.

User Interface

In order to program the user interface for a mobile device you need to understand how mobile apps are used, along with the device's input and display capabilities. Typically when you use a mobile app there's a sense of immediacy; you're using the app for a specific need at that time. As a result to a significant extent the success/failure of a mobile app is dependent upon how quickly it can provide the specific information you need. If the response isn't fast enough, the user isn't going to use the app. To put it another way, when using a device you are not looking to perform complex user interactions that may stretch over a long period of time. This means that the user interface must be designed to enable fast access to the relevant data.

You must also remain aware of the fact that the display screen is considerably smaller (compared to desktop monitors) for tablets, and much smaller for mobile phones and PDAs. There are several things to consider regarding screen size:

- *Information display*
  Due to the smaller screen size there is less information that can be comfortably displayed on the screen. As a result, you should optimize the user interface so that only the most important information is displayed on the screen, with simplified controls (buttons, tabs, etc.) for user input. For most mobile device platforms, in general only one application screen is displayed at a time. An app can have as many different screens as necessary, but they are displayed sequentially, not simultaneously. Your app can use multiple views and/or split views in conjunction with view navigation controls to present the right data to the user in the right context.
- *Information layout*
  The layout of information should also be optimized for the screen size. Hierarchical display of data enables you to minimize/eliminate screen clutter, potentially improve application performance, and also provide a better flow to the application.
- *Navigation*
  View navigation is especially important for mobile interfaces because of the limited space and constrained interactions. Mobile apps cannot be opened in multiple tabs, use keyboard shortcuts, or create macros, so it's vital that every part of your app be easy to access. Common UI elements used to control view presentation include navigation controls, tab bars, toolbars, split views, and popover elements.

Mobile devices have several options for user input. Although some have an actual keyboard, it has become more common for the devices to primarily employ touch screen technology and a virtual keyboard. When you design a user interface for a mobile device, there are several things to consider regarding user input:

- *Input speed*
  Even with mobile devices that have an actual (miniature) keyboard, input speed is less than that possible with a full keyboard. The user input should be designed to require minimal/no keyboard input where

possible. Now some mobile computing platforms provide support for voice recognition and dictation and/or pen and handwriting recognition; if available these can also be incorporated into your user interface design where appropriate.

- *Input precision*
  User input with touch screen technology is not as precise as that provided with a mouse; in addition touch screens lack a visible pointer/cursor. As a result you must design the user interface to operate properly with less accurate input. For example the spacing between input controls (buttons, etc.) needs to be enough to minimize selection errors, while still fitting properly on the smaller display.

- *Input controls*
  Whereas a mouse input device may have multiple controls and/or a scroll wheel, a touch screen supports touch input with one or more fingers. Hence the number and type of input triggers a program receives from touch screen input are different from that received by mouse input. Now many touch screens also provide gesture recognition. You should design the user interface to take advantage of these features. For example contextual menus, tool tips, and other effects that are easy to produce using a mouse, must be implemented differently for touch screens.

Resource Constraints

Even though mobile devices continue to get more powerful and feature-packed; they are still resource-constrained compared to laptop and desktop computers. Specifically, devices are typically not expandable (you can't add memory, storage, etc.) and have a relatively limited battery life between charges. From a programming perspective, this means that you should write your app to minimize use of computing resources (e.g. memory, disk, networking devices, camera, GPS, accelerometers, etc.). Doing this will reduce both resource usage and power consumption. Also be aware that a mobile app may need to be shut down due to resource limitations (low battery, low memory) or upon user request. As a result, if your mobile app creates or modifies data that needs to be saved, it must be able to do this quickly, or risk the loss of this data.

Network Connectivity

Mobile devices have extensive capabilities for connecting to networks, such as mobile (3G, 4G, etc.), Wi-Fi, and Bluetooth technologies. As these are all wireless technologies, network speed, availability, and reliability is variable. Hence, to the extent possible, you should write your mobile apps to be able to operate with limited or no network connectivity. This means that you should try to minimize both the amount of data sent over the network and the frequency of network transmissions.

Security

Mobile networks have various levels of security. Many Wi-Fi networks are public or insecure, meaning that any device or user can connect them. Unsecured networks do not provide any privacy – information sent over an unsecured network can be read or modified by anyone connected to it. In addition, many of the security mechanisms provided for Wi-Fi networks do not provide strong security and can be easily defeated. As a result if your mobile app transmits data over a network, you must *encrypt* this data to make it readable only by the intended recipient(s).

Most mobile device platforms restrict what resources on the device your programs can access and also insure user data isn't shared between apps. For example, each mobile app may have its own private storage for data, mobile apps may only be allowed to read and write files on a device in certain locations, mobile apps have constraints on network access, etc. As these restrictions and constraints are different for each mobile platform, you must understand those of the target device and write your app accordingly.

Developing a Mobile App

Other key factors to consider when developing a mobile app are the application architecture and design approach, and the mobile device platform(s) the app will run on. Next we'll examine these in more detail to understand the issues involved.

Design Approach

When you develop a mobile app you have several application design approaches to choose from: mobile web app, native app, or hybrid app. A **mobile web app** is a website designed to function in an app-like way. Mobile web apps run in a web browser on a device; for example an iOS web application runs inside the built-in Safari browser installed on Apple iOS devices.

You develop this type of application using web technologies, such as HTML, CSS, JavaScript, and AJAX. A **mobile native app** runs on a device-specific platform, such as iOS or Android. Native apps can access all the capabilities of the device. You develop this type of application using a language supported by the platform, for example Objective-C or Java. A **mobile hybrid app** runs inside the device web browser but also integrates with the device-specific platform, thereby giving it access to platform-specific functionality. This approach attempts to leverage the benefits of both standards-based web technologies along with the native capabilities of the device.

So, how do you choose the type of app to develop? Each approach has its advantages and disadvantages as summarized here:

- Performance
  The performance of a web app is often less than that of a native app, due to both the programming language being used and also to the fact that web apps operate over a network.
- Offline usage
  Native apps are typically designed to work, at least to some extent, even when the network is not available, whereas web apps require the network to be operational.
- Portability
  Mobile web apps run in the built-in web browser of the device and are developed using standard web technologies. This means that they are generally portable across different mobile devices. If you want to create mobile applications for multiple devices, it is much easier to do with web apps.
- Accessibility
  As mobile web apps run within the device browser they are simple to access (don't have to be downloaded). Native and hybrid apps are typically accessed from an online application distribution, such as the Apple App Store or the Google Android market.
- Findability
  As mobile web apps are in fact web sites, a search engine is typically all that's needed to find and use the app. Native and hybrid apps, on the other hand, are typically available through the appropriate distribution site. Any developer can submit their native app to the

site, where users can discover it through a combination of browsing, searching, and getting recommendations.

- Device attributes
  Native apps typically have more and better use of specific features of a device (e.g. GPS, cameras, accelerometers, side buttons, etc.).
- Monetization
  Native apps provide multiple channels for generating revenue - direct charge, in-app payment, subscription, ads, sponsorship, etc. As of the present, mobile web apps have fewer mature mechanisms for generating revenue.

The factors mentioned above can be important in determining the design approach for developing a mobile app. Of course other constraints or concerns (for example, you have experience developing native apps, etc.) may be important as well. Whatever the scenario, you now have an understanding of some of the key tradeoffs in choosing your design approach.

Mobile Device Platforms

A mobile device platform provides a full suite of tools for mobile application development. This includes programming language support, an IDE, application testing tools, and other features. In order to familiarize you with some common features of these platforms, we'll spend the next few paragraphs looking at the iOS and Android platforms.

iOS Platform

The iOS mobile platform comprises the operating system, software infrastructure, and tools for developing and running apps on Apple iOS devices (iPod, iPhone, iPad). The following diagram depicts this architecture.

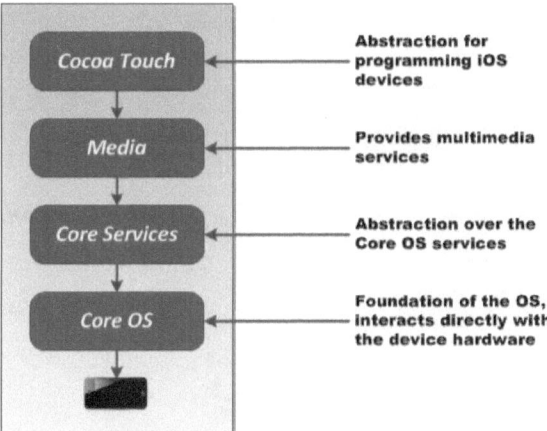

Figure 28. iOS Platform

Working from the actual device up, the *Core OS* technologies contain the low-level features that the other technologies are built upon. This includes a set of core software libraries and the operating system. The *Core Services* technologies provide networking configuration and support, data modeling, data management and services, use of location-based technologies (GPS, Wi-Fi, cell), media services, telephony, and other services. The *Media* technologies comprise graphics, audio, and video technologies. The *Cocoa Touch* technologies contain the key software libraries that developers use for building iOS applications.

The iOS platform includes the Xcode tools (Xcode IDE, Instruments) for developing native apps on the iOS platform using the Objective-C, C, and C++ programming languages.

Android Platform
The Android mobile platform comprises the operating system, software infrastructure, and tools for developing and running apps on Android-compliant mobile devices.

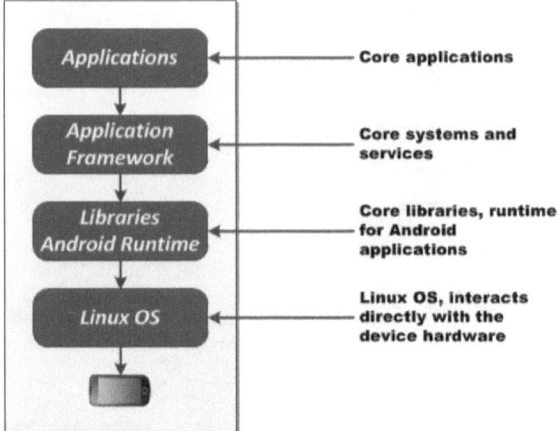

Figure 29. Android Platform

The *Linux OS* technologies are the Linux-based operating system kernel, consisting of hardware device drivers, memory management, process management, and networking support. The libraries and Android runtime includes the core libraries and runtime for Android applications. The libraries support windowing, multimedia, data management, and browser. The Android runtime is the virtual machine (optimized for mobile devices) and core Java libraries for executing Android applications. The *Application Framework* includes the core systems and services for developing Android applications. Android applications are developed using Java and is supported by numerous IDEs.

Your First iPhone App
Now comes the fun part, you're going to develop your first iPhone app! You'll need an Intel-based Mac computer with OS X Lion (or later) installed to perform this exercise; if you don't have one or simply choose not to create this program yourself, you can follow along and note the steps involved. Here's a look at the finished app we'll be developing

Figure 30. Greeting iPhone App

As you can see this is a very basic app that just displays a simple greeting. It's meant to introduce you to several key components of the iOS development environment and how they are used to build applications. OK, so let's get started!

Create a Project

As noted in the chapter *The Programmer's Toolkit*, Xcode 4 is the tool used to develop iOS (e.g. iPhone/iPad/iPod) applications. Once you have downloaded and installed Xcode 4 (as discussed in the Programmer's Toolkit chapter), launch the program and the welcome window is displayed.

(Note: If you have an iOS device (e.g. iPhone/iPod/iPad), then don't connect it to the computer. In this exercise we'll be using the *iOS Simulator* to run this program in lieu of deploying it to a device.)

Programming for Everyone

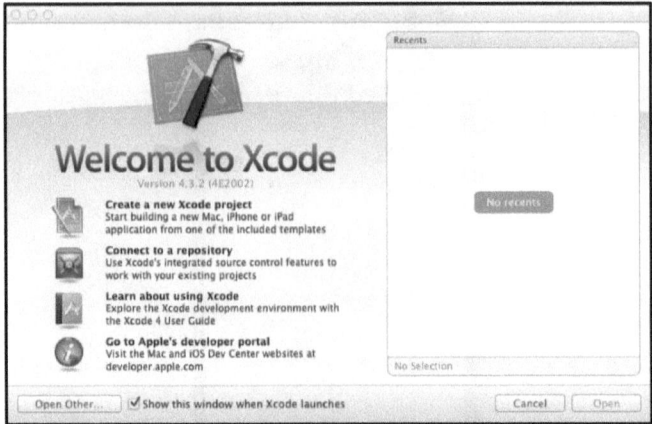

Figure 31. Xcode Welcome Window

From this window a variety of options are presented, let's select the **Create a new Xcode project** option (Note that you can also create a new project by selecting **File → New → New Project ...** from the Xcode menu). Once you have selected this option the Xcode Project Template window is displayed.

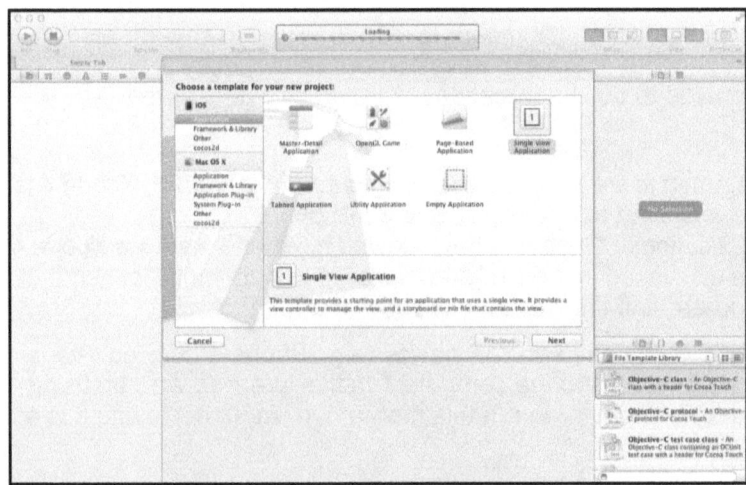

Figure 32. Xcode Project Template

In the project template window you can specify the type of app you'll develop; Xcode provides several templates that can be used as a starting point. The example app has a single screen; hence we'll use the *Single View Application* template for it. In the window click **Application** under the iOS label in the upper left side of the window, then click the **Single View Application** icon on the right side of the window (the type of application we'll be developing), and finally click the **Next** button. A window is then displayed for configuring project options.

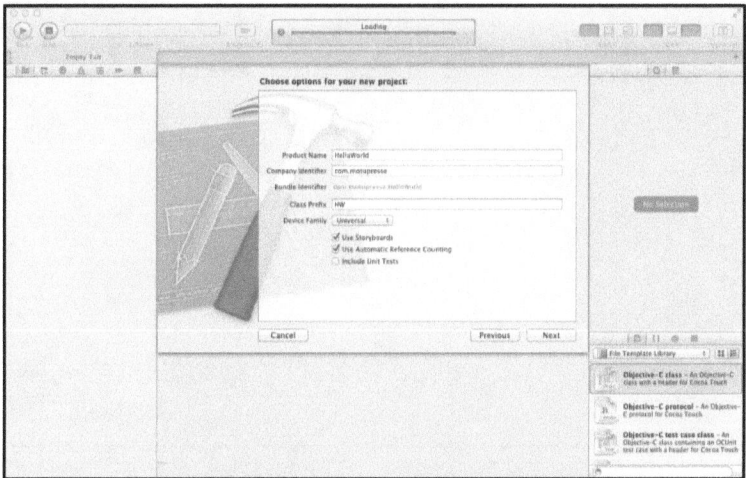

Figure 33. Xcode Project Options Window

In the project options window you should enter values for the following options:

- Product Name - your new product name. Xcode uses this to name the project; here *HelloWorld* is entered but you can type a different name if you prefer.
- Company Identifier – this is a text string used to identify who made the application. You should enter a unique identifier (e.g. company name); if you don't have a company you can just enter *edu.self*. Here *com.motupresse* is entered.
- Class Prefix - a prefix that Xcode uses to name all created classes it creates. The prefix is added to class names to avoid naming conflicts; here *HW* is entered.
- Device Family - the device family to create the app for running on an iPhone, iPod Touch, or iPad. A Universal app will run on all iOS devices, so we have selected that here.

There are three checkboxes at the bottom of this window; make sure to select *Use Storyboards* and *Use Automatic Reference Counting* and deselect *Include Unit Tests*. After you have done this click the **Next** button to continue onto the window that allows you to specify the location where you want to store your project files.

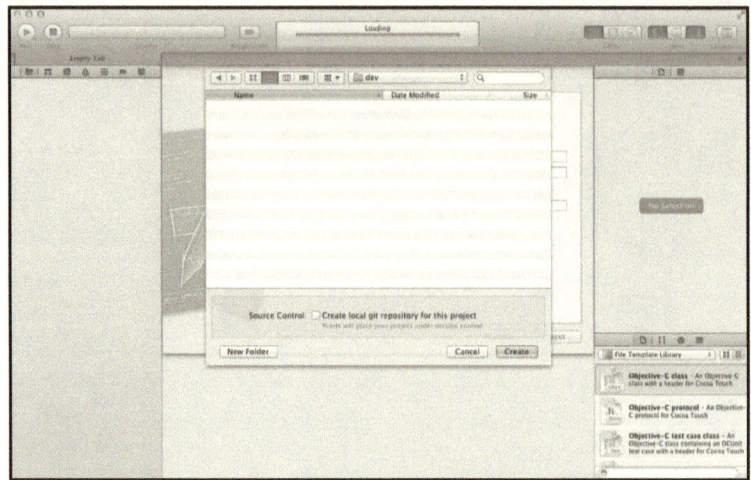

Figure 34. Xcode Project Folder Window

Select a location on your computer; you can use the current folder, select a different folder, or create a new folder (using the **New Folder** button) for the files. Make sure you do not check the **Source Control** checkbox; and when you are done click the **Create** button to finish creating the project. The Xcode Workspace Window is then displayed.

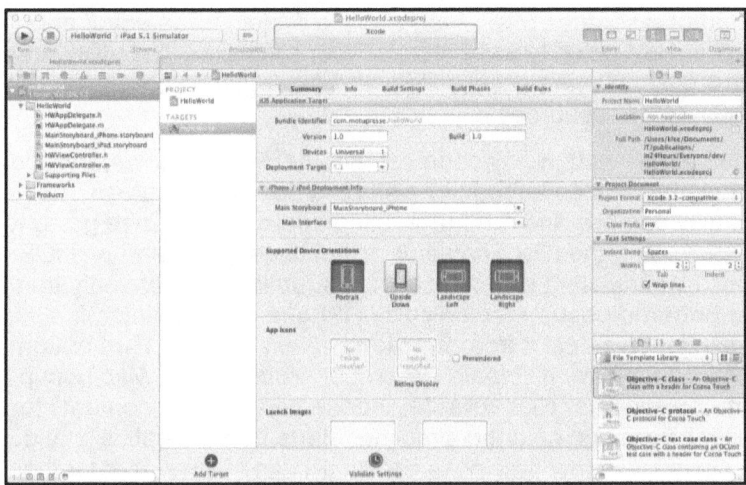

Figure 35. Xcode Workspace Window

The workspace window is divided into a toolbar that extends horizontally across the top of the window and three areas below it divided into columns that take up the remainder of the window.

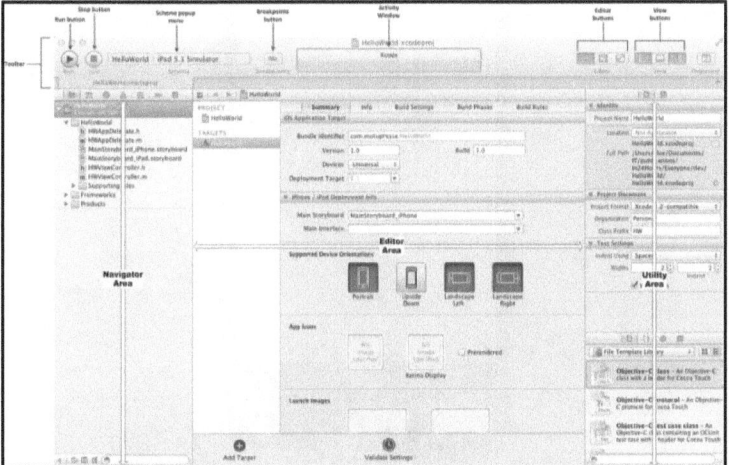

Figure 36. Xcode Workspace Window Elements

The toolbar includes the **Run** and **Stop** buttons, a **Scheme** popup menu, a **Breakpoints** button, **Editor** buttons, **View** buttons, and an **Organizer** button. The 3 areas below the toolbar comprise the Navigator area, the Editor area, and the Utility area. The navigator area is used to view and access different resources (files, etc.) within a project. The editor area is where you'll actually write most of your program. The utility area is used to view and access Help and other inspectors and to use ready-made resources in your project.

You haven't written any code yet, but the *Single View Application* template provides enough of a starting point that you can actually compile and run the existing application. We're going to do that using the *iOS Simulator*, a tool used to run and test iOS apps by simulating iOS devices. Let's run it now; first verify that the **Scheme** popup menu displays iPhone 5.0 Simulator, if it doesn't then select it from the menu. Next click the **Run** button from the toolbar. If *Enable Developer Mode on this Mac* popup window appears, click **Enable**. Xcode takes a few moments to build the project; next the simulator starts up automatically and displays a window that looks like an iPhone. The simulator then opens your app, which should look like this:

Figure 37. Skeleton Hello World App

As you can see, your app displays a blank white screen. The *Single View Application* template creates the skeleton for your app, enough so that all you have to do is fill in the details (program code, visual content, etc.). We'll start doing that next, but for now quit the simulator by choosing **iOS Simulator ➜ Quit iOS Simulator** from the Xcode menu.

Add UI Elements to the View

If you look at the Navigator area of the workspace window, at the top you'll see a selector bar comprised of seven buttons and below that the main navigator area. Click the leftmost button to see the project navigator view.

Figure 38. Xcode Main Navigator Area

The project navigator view displays all the files in the project. Notice the *HelloWorld* folder; the file we want to edit is within this folder. Open the folder by clicking the *disclosure* triangle to the left of it; the triangle will point down and its files will be displayed. Now select the *MainStoryboard_iPhone.storyboard* file by clicking it. Notice that Xcode opens the storyboard in the editor area.

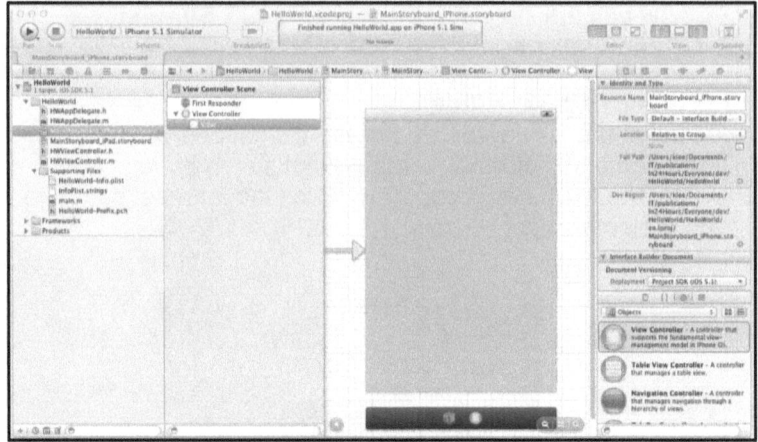

Figure 39. Hello World Editor View Area

As shown in the figure above, the key elements of the editor area are the outline view, canvas, scene, scene indicator, and scene dock.

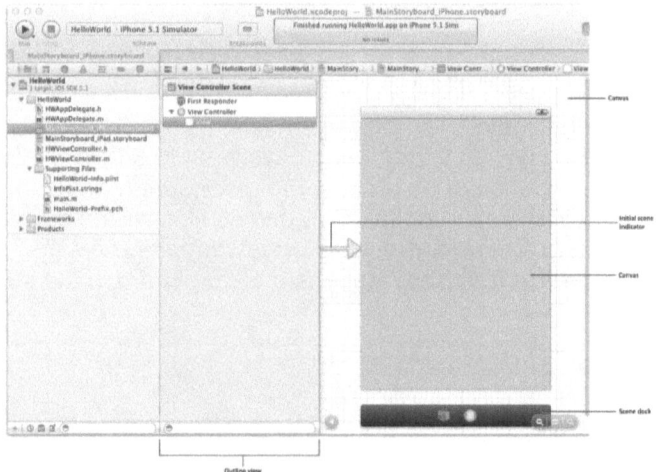

Figure 40. Editor Area

A storyboard is a visual representation of the user interface of an iOS application. It contains the contents of each screen, or *scene*, along with the transition, or *segue*, between scenes. Programmatically each scene is comprised of a *view controller* (an Objective-C class that manages a scene) and one or more *views* (graphical view elements, e.g. tables, text, buttons, etc).

Now let's look at the view elements of the scene. Notice in the outline view (titled *View Controller Scene*) two items – *First Responder* and *View Controller*. Observe that there is a disclosure triangle to the left of the view controller. Open the view controller scene (by clicking the disclosure triangle) to see its current content, you will see one view object named *View*.

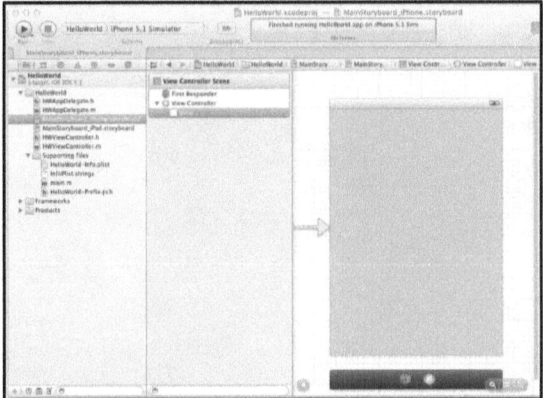

Figure 41. Hello World View Object

The view controller manages all of the content of a scene. The content may include multiple items, such as view objects, labels, buttons, tables, etc. Now let's use the object library to add a label to the view; a label is used to display text. First select the view (by clicking the View icon below the view controller). The object library is at the bottom of the utilities area on the right side of the Xcode window. Click the third button from the left in the library selection bar to open the object library.

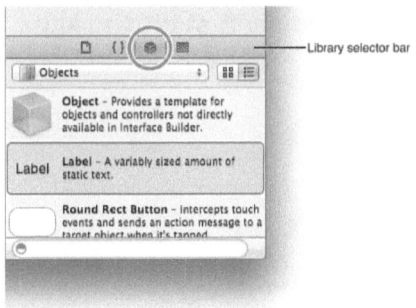

Figure 42. Object Library

The object library is a collection of elements provided by Xcode for building user interfaces. Instead of writing code, you use the object library to drag-and-drop UI elements onto the view. You can also move and edit these objects as desired. Scroll through the library until you find the *Label* object. Drag a label from the list and drop it onto the view object on the canvas; it will have default text of **Label**. Place the label anywhere you like on the canvas by dragging and dropping it accordingly. Now double-click the label object and change its text to **Hello, World!**

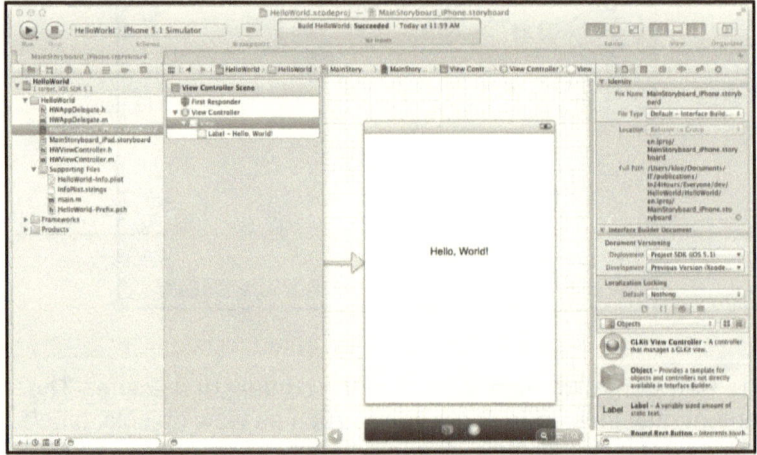

Figure 43. Adding the First Label to the App

OK, we have added the first label to our app; before we go any further let's save our program by selecting **File ➔ Save** from the Xcode menu. Next let's add the second label to the app repeating the actions performed for the first label; this time change the text to **This is my first iPhone app**.

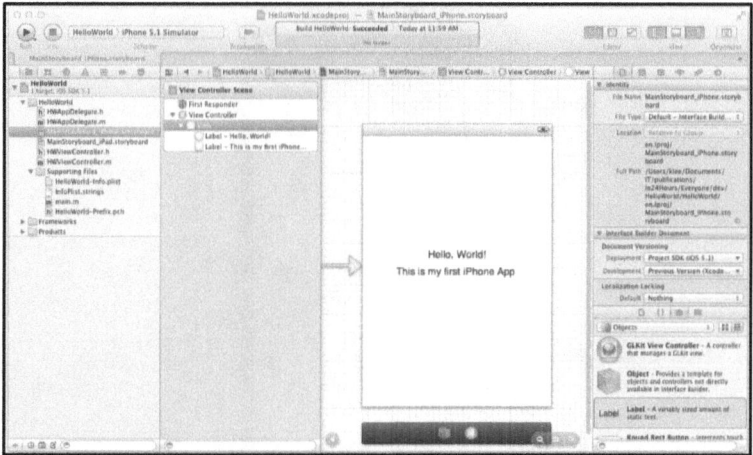

Figure 44. Adding a Second Label to the App

Save your program; thanks to Xcode you have now added all of the view elements for your app without writing a single line of code!

Test Your App
Now let's build and run the app; as before click the **Run** button from the toolbar. After a few moments you should see the following in the simulator.

Figure 45. Your First iPhone App, the Finished Product

Congratulations, you have completed your first iPhone App! You now have a better understanding of how the Xcode IDE tools along with the iOS platform help to simplify mobile app development. Similar tools are provided for the other leading mobile platforms, so no matter which one you pick, you should be able to quickly get started building apps for your device.

Summary

This has been a pretty detailed introduction to mobile app development so thanks for sticking with me through this. You now have a good general overview of mobile device programming, and also some hands-on experience with the basics of developing iPhone apps. As you can imagine, there's a lot more to learn if you want to develop sophisticated mobile apps, and there are plenty of resources listed in the **References** Appendix that can provide you with help. So what are you waiting for, start creating your own mobile apps and don't look back!

Chapter 10
Secure Coding

Computer systems and programs are used every day to manage your personal information. If even one of these has security vulnerabilities, then your information is at risk. When the systems and programs that manage your data are vulnerable, it's like leaving an entry door unlocked or an exterior window open in your house. The risks for information theft are multiplied because potentially many more people (millions if the information is available online) can exploit computer program vulnerabilities. Every program is a potential target; attackers will try to find security vulnerabilities in your applications or computer systems. They'll then try to exploit these vulnerabilities to steal secrets, corrupt programs and data, and even gain control of entire computer systems and networks.

Figure 46. Computer Hacker at Work

Secure coding is the practice of writing programs that are resistant to attack by malicious or mischievous people or programs. Secure coding helps protect a user's data from theft or corruption. It can also help prevent unwanted access to computers and the programs that run on them.

Security is important for all software and isn't something that is added after the fact; secure coding is something you need to do for every program that you develop. This chapter provides an overview of computer security, why secure programming is so important, and identifies some of the steps you can take to write more secure code.

Overview
Let's start by establishing a common understanding of security. To the general user, computer security is a set of mechanisms that insure

- Your information is secure, meaning that your information is accessible by authorized users and protected from unauthorized access.
- Your computer system is secure, meaning that your computer and the programs that reside on it are available and protected from unauthorized access or unwanted behavior.

Most computer systems, including those that host websites and programs, run in a "low security operating environment". This means that the systems themselves do not provide a high level of security and hence you are responsible for making your programs secure. Your software must be resistant to attacks over a network and attacks by people sitting at the computer keyboard – you can't just rely on firewalls and passwords to protect you. In order to do this you have to identify the key threats that cause software security vulnerabilities and then incorporate secure coding practices to protect your systems and programs from these attacks.

Software Vulnerabilities

There are a variety of causes for software security vulnerabilities, but in general we can say that most are due to program errors. If a programmer leaves a bug in a program that can be exploited, an attacker may discover this bug and take advantage of it. Some of the most common software vulnerabilities are:

- *Buffer overflows*
  A buffer is a portion of computer memory used to temporarily store data while it is being moved from one place to another. An example of how buffers are used is when you stream a YouTube video; the YouTube player may create a buffer for transferring the content. A buffer overflow occurs when a program attempts to write data past the end (or, occasionally, past the beginning) of a buffer; if this occurs the program can potentially overwrite the data of another program. This can result in data corruption, program crashes or incorrect operation. It can also provide an attacker a means to gain control of your computer – for example an attacker can use this technique to insert malicious code that is then executed, potentially taking complete control of your system. If you are using a programming language that has no built-in protection against buffer overflows, then you must provide these checks within your program.
- *Incorrect/no input data validation*
  Any input to your programs from an untrusted source is a potential means for your program/system to be attacked. From a computer and information security perspective, any user should be considered an untrusted source; hence your programs should validate all input

data. In this context validate means that your program should verify that input data is the correct type and size, and within the expected ranges. For example if a program is designed to process numeric input values in the range 0 to 1000 it should verify the input is within that range before processing it. If your program does not validate input data then errors may occur later during processing, potentially causing a security hole.

- *Race conditions*
  A race condition is when changes to the order of two or more events can cause a change in the behavior of a program. If an attacker can take advantage of the situation to insert malicious code, change a filename, or otherwise interfere with the normal operation of the program, you have a security vulnerability. Attackers can sometimes take advantage of small time gaps in the processing of code to interfere with the sequence of operations, which they then exploit.

- *Privilege problems*
  An important aspect of computer security is protecting computer systems and information from unauthorized access and use. If a user can gain more privileges on a system than he should have, a security vulnerability exists. Some software bugs can cause privilege confusion or privilege escalation that enable an attacker to gain elevated privileges. Websites must also perform access control checks each time pages are accessed in order to prevent attackers from gaining access to protected pages.

Security Risks

So, how do these vulnerabilities translate to computer security issues that we face every day? The table below shows the relationships by mapping the software vulnerabilities defined above to some common security risks.

Software Bugs			
Buffer Overflow	**Input Validation Error**	**Race Condition**	**Privilege Problem**
Security Risks Stack buffer overflow Heap overflow Buffer underflow	Format string attacks SQL injection Email injection Code injection Cross-site scripting HTTP header injection Unvalidated redirects and forwards	Time-of-check to time-of-use bugs	Cross-site request forgery Clickjacking FTP bounce attack Failure to restrict URL access Broken authentication and session management Insecure direct object references

Table 4. Common Security Risks

Attacks due to the above security risks cost users and business millions of dollars every year. In the next section we'll look at some secure coding practices you can implement to manage these risks.

Secure Coding Practices

The secure coding practices documented in the following paragraphs are meant to cover many common scenarios when you are developing programs. Note that some of this is pretty technical and may not be relevant for the programming you're doing right now, but in any case you should review these recommendations and apply them if/when necessary.

Validating Input

Proper input validation can eliminate the vast majority of software vulnerabilities. Therefore your programs should validate all external data sources, including text input fields, command line arguments, commands passed through a URL used to launch a your programs, media files provided by users or other programs, network interfaces, environmental variables. For example, let's say that we added a form to the greeting web page we wrote earlier; this form will be used to request the user's name and use this input to generate a response. The following simple JavaScript function named **validateGreeting** checks if the field `gForm` for the form `name` is not empty.

```
function validateGreeting()
{
  var x=document.forms["gForm"]["name"].value;
  if ((x==null) || (x==""))
  {
    alert("Please provide name");
    return false;
  }
}
```

We can modify the web page to call this function when the form is submitted. If the field is empty an alert box is presented to the user.

Now you may be wondering, "I see that I can put in checks to make sure that a user doesn't provide invalid input data, but how are these checks protecting my computer and its programs"? Well, as you'll see in the next few sections, the input of bad data can cause a program to fail, and an attacker can exploit the consequences of this failure as a means of taking control of a system. Thus it is vital that your programs (and web pages) validate input data.

Protect Against Buffer Overflows

A buffer is a region of computer memory used to temporarily hold data when it is being moved from one place to another. A buffer overflow is an error whereby a program, while writing data to a buffer, overflows the buffer's boundary, Buffer overflows are a major source of security vulnerabilities in the C and C++ programming languages. This is because these languages have library functions with no built-in checks for text string length, and they also do not enforce *bounds checking*. For example, the C language has a function named `strcpy` which is used for copying a string to a variable. In the following code fragment

```
char destination[4];
char *source = "Malicious Code!";
strcpy(destination, source);
```

The `destination` variable is an array (an ordered collection of values or variables) that holds up to 4 characters, hence if you use `strcpy` to copy the `source` text string (which is more than

4 characters) to the `destination` variable an overflow will occur, overwriting the memory after that allocated for the variable. *Bounds checking* is a method of detecting whether a variable is within some bounds before its use. When performed on arrays it detects if an array element you are trying to access is within the size of the array. Since the C and C++ languages don't perform array bounds checking, if the following line is added to the above code example

```
char badValue = destination[10];
```

A buffer overflow would occur because the code is trying to access a value outside the bounds of the `destination` array. With this in mind here are several recommendations that you should follow to protect against buffer overflows:

- When you have a choice, only use *safe* functions (those which have built-in checks for buffer length when copying data).
- When working with fixed-length buffers, calculate the size of the source buffer, and don't put more data in the destination buffer than it can hold.
- Perform checks to make sure integer numbers input or computed are not larger than that allowed. When you create a variable for a number in a program, you specify its type (e.g. integer, real), its sign (positive and negative values, or positive only), and its size (i.e. the maximum size of a number). These parameters affect how much memory is allocated for it. If, after creating a variable, you attempt to store a value in it that is greater than the amount of memory allocated for it, an overflow occurs. It is also possible for a computed value to be larger than the size supported by the destination variable. To avoid these errors your program should include checks to make sure integer overflow has not occurred before storing a value.

Prevent Injection Attacks
An injection attack is a technique used to insert malicious code into a computer program to change its execution. A program processing invalid data causes these bugs. They often work by getting a user to perform an unintended action, enabling an attacker to perform actions under the guise of the unaware user or obtain a user's confidential information. For websites the malicious code is often in the form of JavaScript that executes

when the user clicks a link of loads a page. For example,
suppose you create a web page with an input field requesting
user comments that also displays the submitted comment; if the
input field is named `comment` then it can be displayed with the
following JavaScript.

```
<span id="query">
  <%=Request.QueryString["comment"]%>
</span>
```

This type of page is common on a bulletin board type of website,
for example one that enables you to enter and view customer
feedback. Now if you enter a text comment, for example "I like
your products", then this will be displayed on the website using
the above JavaScript. However, if the comment is a JavaScript
code fragment, then the code will actually be executed! The
problem with this is that a malicious user can take advantage of
this vulnerability to insert JavaScript code that can exploit this
(e.g. steal browser cookies or form data, etc.). Once an
unsuspecting user views this website, the malicious JavaScript
code would run and potentially send the user's personal data to
another website.

There are various methods to prevent injection attacks; in
general they all involve some type of input data validation and/or
filtering.

Default Deny
Your programs should be designed such that, *by default* access
is denied to resources and permission is required in order for
access to be granted. This approach is more secure because it
is typically impossible to know, in advance, whether an
unknown/unrecognized user/request/etc. is malicious. In general
your programs should base access decisions on permissions.

Sanitize Data Sent to Other Systems
Your programs should sanitize all data passed to other systems.
Attackers may be able to invoke unused functionality in these
systems through injection attacks. Because your programs
understand the context in which they are accessing these
systems, they are responsible for sanitizing the data prior to
access.

Adopt a Secure Coding Standard

Develop and/or apply a secure coding standard for your target development language and platform. Many of the programming languages in use today have a published set of guidelines and/or recommendations for secure software development in the language, so you should become very familiar with these as you write your programs.

Divide, Test, and Conquer

It was mentioned earlier that program errors are the main source of software security vulnerabilities. Hence developing high quality, bug-free software will lead to much more secure software. A proven way to achieve these goals is the use of iterative, incremental, test-centric software development practices. This means developing small portions of a software system incrementally, in repeated cycles (iteratively), in order to build the system up over time. This software development practice is test-centric, meaning that each development cycle is centered on tests that specify the desired function and behavior for the software, and (are run to) validate that the software has been correctly implemented. The general approach is summarized as follows:

1. Determine functionality and/or behavior you want the system to exhibit.
2. Create one or more tests that will validate the expected behavior.
3. Implement the software.
4. Run the test(s) and verify that the expected and actual results match.

There are a variety of tools and frameworks available today that can be used to facilitate adoption of these software development practices.

Summary

Software security is extremely important – the number of security related incidents shows no signs of decreasing, despite the various measures that have been taking to make software and computer systems more secure. It is very important to adopt policies that can make your data and systems less prone to being compromised. You now have a general understanding of some basic steps you can take to make your software more secure; you should apply these whenever you write programs.

Chapter 11
Computer Graphics

Computer graphics programming includes image creation and manipulation, animation, and computer-generated imagery (CGI). Developments in computer graphics have revolutionized media and modern visual arts. Just consider this: much of the content you see today – whether in films, on television, or as media, is created using some form of computer graphics. In this chapter you will get an overview of how computer graphics are used, learn about some of the common tools for developing graphics, and then roll up your sleeves and create a few simple computer graphics yourself!

Basic Elements of a Digital Image
When we talk about computer graphics, we need to understand how digital images are represented, created, and manipulated by a computer. To get started on this, we'll begin by reviewing the main concepts and ideas around digital imaging, image rendering, and image modeling.

Image Data
A digital image is, simply put, a numeric representation of an image. Digital images may be captured by devices such as cameras, or created and rendered by computer graphics technology. A digital image is typically encoded as binary data and stored in a file. Although there are several digital image types, the most common is the *raster graphics* (aka bitmap)

image type. A raster graphics image is a rectangular grid of picture elements (pixels) that can be viewed on a supported display medium (e.g. a monitor, a piece of paper [for a printout], etc.). Each pixel holds one or more values that represent the brightness of a given color(s) at a specified point. The *size*, or number of bits per pixel, determines the number of colors a pixel can represent, and potentially its transparency. For a color graphic, a pixel has three values that represent RGB data values. The RGB color model represents the amount of red, green and blue light combined together to produce a color.

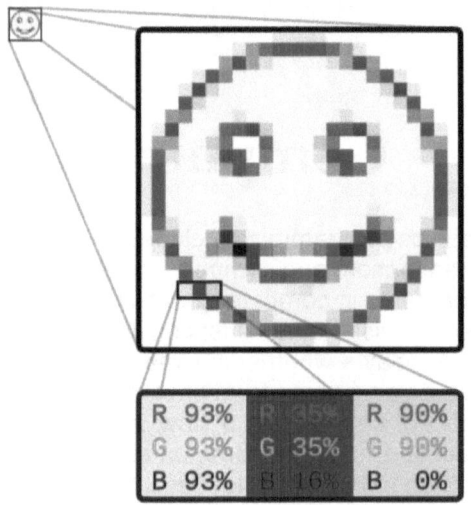

Figure 47. Example Raster Graphics Digital Image

A key characteristic of a raster graphics digital image is its *resolution*, i.e. the amount of detail the image has. The higher the resolution of an image, the more pixels it has and hence the larger the corresponding image data file. There are multiple image file formats used for organizing and storing digital images, each of which has its own specific features. Computer graphics technology is used to create both static digital images with two or three-dimensional representations, and also moving (i.e. *animated*) digital images.

Two-Dimensional Graphics
Two-dimensional (2D) computer graphics is the computer-based generation of images, primarily from two-dimensional models such as 2D geometric models, text, and digital images, and

techniques specific to them. The most common techniques used to create 2D graphics are raster graphics and vector graphics. Raster graphics were discussed in the previous section; vector graphics represent images as an array of pixels, and are commonly used for photographic images.

Three-Dimensional Graphics

A three dimensional (3D) graphic, also known as a 3D model, is a mathematical representation of a three-dimensional object. This geometric data is stored in the computer for the purposes of performing calculations and rendering 2D images. A 3D model is not technically a graphic until it is visually displayed. This model can be projected visually on a medium as a two-dimensional image through a process called *3D rendering*. Computer-generated imagery (CGI) is often used to apply 3D computer graphics to special effects in art, video games, films, television programs, commercials, simulations, and printed media.

Animation

Computer animation is the process used for generating and displaying a sequence of digital images to create an illusion of movement; it is effectively the digital version of traditional animation techniques, such as stop motion techniques and frame-by-frame animation. The target of the animation can be the computer itself, or another medium such as film. Computer animation is created digitally on a computer using the appropriate software and can utilize both 2D and 3D graphics. The most common techniques used to create computer animation include keyframing, motion capture, and kinematics. With keyframing every frame of the computer animation is directly modified or manipulated by the creator, giving you complete control over the animation. This technique is comparable to traditional hand-drawn animation. With motion capture the actions of human actors are recorded and used to animate digital character models. Kinematics is often used for game programming and 3D animation; it involves the use of kinematic equations of motion to determine the position for each frame of animation. Each technique has its pros and cons, and they are often used together to animate a scene depending upon requirements.

Image Modeling

3D image modeling is the process of developing a 3D surface model of any object using software. The model can be displayed as a 2D image using 3D rendering software, used in a computer simulation, or physically created using 3D printing devices. Models can be created automatically or manually, by hand, by algorithm, or scanned. They are used in a wide variety of fields, including the medical industry, film, video games, architecture, earth science, and engineering.

A 3D model represents a collection of points in 3D space, connected by geometric items such as lines, curved surfaces, triangles, etc. Most 3D models are *solid* (define the volume of the object they represent) or *shell/boundary* (represent the perimeter, i.e. exterior of the object). Shell models are easier to work with than solid models, and are the most commonly used in video games and film.

There are three common ways to represent a model: polygonal modeling, curve modeling, and digital sculpting. *Polygonal modeling* is flexible and can be rendered quickly by computer programs; it is the most commonly used technique for creating 3D models. However, polygon models cannot accurately represent curved surfaces.

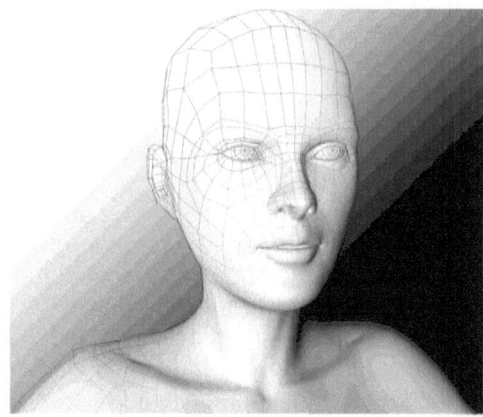

Figure 48. Polygon Model of a Human Face

With *curve modeling* the 3D surfaces are defined by curves. This produces a more accurate rendering of 3D surfaces, but may not be rendered as quickly. *Digital sculpting* software enables you to sculpt (i.e. push, pull, smooth, grab, pinch, etc.) a digital object as if it were made of sculpting material, e.g. clay.

Digital sculpting can make it possible to create details in a model not possible with the other techniques, thus providing photorealistic results when rendered.

Image Rendering

Rendering is the process of generating a 2D image or animation from a prepared scene. The scene, also known as the *model*, is a description of (view) objects; it contains geometry, viewpoint, texture, and lighting information. Rendering may be 2D or 3D, where 3D rendering converts a 3D model into 2D images. 3D rendering can be a complex process; the challenge is using the appropriate techniques to project 3D models (which have height, width, and depth) onto a flat, 2D display device. The steps involved in 3D rendering require both determining which parts of a scene to show on the display and how each pixel on the display should look for maximum realism. These effects are best obtained by careful consideration of the surface textures involved (including their colors and reflectance), lighting (shading and shadows of images), view perspective, anti-aliasing (smoothes out rough edges of images), and the depth-of-field desired.

Many image rendering techniques have been created and analyzed; those commonly in use are rasterization, ray casting, ray tracing, and radiosity. *Rasterization*, the method used by all current graphics cards, considers the objects in the scene and projects them to form an image, with no facility for generating a point-of-view perspective effect. *Ray casting* considers the scene as observed from a specific point-of-view, calculating the observed image based only on geometry and very basic optical laws of reflection intensity. *Ray tracing* is similar to ray casting, but employs more advanced optical simulation and usually uses advanced techniques to obtain more realistic results at a speed that is often orders of magnitude slower. *Radiosity* calculates the passage of light as it leaves the light source and illuminates surfaces. These surfaces are usually rendered to the display using one of the other three techniques. There are a variety of factors important to determining which technique to choose, including realism, performance, and resource utilization. Computer graphics software packages often combine two or more of the above techniques to obtain the best results.

Languages and Libraries

Computer graphics programming is most commonly done using graphics libraries, platforms, and specialized programming languages. There are numerous options available for image creation and manipulation, CGI, and computer animation. Many also support importing existing images (perhaps created using equipment such as digital cameras or scanners) and then manipulating them as desired. Of course, we can't go over all of the options in this space but you're encouraged to look online or at the resources in the **References** Appendix for more information on specific graphics tools. In the meantime the next few paragraphs provide a brief overview of several graphics programming packages available today.

OpenGL

OpenGL, one of the most popular graphics libraries, is an API for creating 2D and 3D computer graphics. It is intended for use with computer hardware designed and optimized for displaying and manipulating graphics, although *software-only* implementations have also been created. OpenGL is a *procedural* graphics API. What this means is that, instead of describing how something should appear, you use the APIs to prescribe the steps necessary to achieve a certain appearance or effect. The API consists of over 250 different functions that can be used to draw complex three-dimensional scenes, from functions that create anything from simple points, lines, and polygons up to complex lighting and shading, texture mapping, blending, and other effects. As its name implies, OpenGL is an open standard; its API has been implemented for numerous platforms in numerous programming languages. There are also numerous extensions to OpenGL, such as OpenGL ES, a subset of the API designed for embedded systems and mobile devices.

Java 2D

Java 2D is an API for drawing two-dimensional and graphics using the Java programming language. Functionally, Java 2D drawing operations are performed by: 1) creating a shape object, 2) modifying the drawing parameters, and 3) drawing an outlined or solid image of the shape. The Java 2D API supports a variety of standard two-dimensional geometric shapes such as lines, ellipses, and quadrilaterals, and enables the creation of custom shapes. The drawing parameter transformations include setting the paint color or pattern, setting the stroke thickness, setting the font, and performing a coordinate system translation or rotation. Java 2D is interoperable with OpenGL; this enables the two APIs to be used together in Java programs to create graphics.

Processing

Processing is an open-source programming language and development environment used to create computer graphics, animations, and interactions. It can be used on Windows, Mac, and Linux-based computers. Graphics created with processing can be saved in many standard formats. Animations and interactions may be exported to run on the Web or as standalone applications. The capabilities of the platform continue to be extended by the Processing community, which has written over seventy libraries to facilitate computer vision, data visualization, music, networking, and electronics.

Creating Graphics Using Processing

Now that we've completed this introduction on a few of the many possibilities for computer graphics programming, it's time to round out the chapter by getting some hands-on experience. This means creating some images and a simple animation as well; the tool we'll use for this is the **Processing** platform. We'll start off by providing a brief overview of Processing and identifying its main features. Next we'll download and install the software. Finally we'll create a couple of graphics; the first will have animation and the second will employ 3D graphics rendered with OpenGL.

Processing Development Environment

Processing was conceived as a language for artists. It is built on the Java programming language, but uses a simplified syntax and a visual, graphics-based programming model. A Processing program is created in a project called a *sketch*. Each sketch is written with the Processing text editor in its own folder. In the sketch you write the code to create and manipulate graphics, perform animations, etc. A sketch folder can also contain other folders for media files and code libraries.

A sketch is created on a display window with dimensions that you specify using the `size()` function. The window corresponds to the drawing grid, and is specified with two or three dimensions. Processing currently supports five graphics renderers – **JAVA2D** (the default renderer), **P2D** (a fast 2D renderer, but lower quality than the Java 2D renderer), **P3D** (a fast 3D renderer, but lower quality than OpenGL), **OPENGL** (a fast, high quality 3D renderer that uses OpenGL compatible graphics hardware if available), and **PDF** (draws 2D graphics directly to a PDF file). The rendering mode is also specified using the `size()` function. For example, to specify a display window 100 pixels wide and 100 pixels high, that uses the OpenGL renderer, the `size()` function would be programmed as

```
size(100, 100, OPENGL);
```

Windows, Grids, and Coordinates

Processing uses the Cartesian coordinate system for specifying the location of graphics elements in a drawing window. A point on a 2D Cartesian coordinate plane is specified with a numerical pair of coordinates that specify the distance from the point to the plane (for Processing the origin of the window is the upper-left corner). For example, if the drawing window size is specified as 10 pixels wide and 5 pixels high, coordinate (0, 0) is the upper-left pixel and coordinate (9, 4) is in the lower-right. The four points (0, 0), (9, 0), (0, 4), and (9, 4) are shown in the figure provided below.   The last visible pixel in the lower-right corner of the screen is at position (9, 4) because pixels are drawn to the right and below the coordinate.

Figure 49. Processing Window Grid

When drawing in three dimensions, at the surface of the image the z-coordinate is zero, with negative z-values moving back in space. In effect the "camera" is positioned in the center of the screen.

Rendering and Order of Execution

Processing code is executed sequentially and hence the order of the code statements determines how objects are rendered. For example, to draw a black circle, 10-pixels in diameter at location (50, 50) on the screen, you could write the following code

```
fill(0);
ellipse(50, 50, 10, 10);
```

The fill() function sets the color used to fill all subsequent shapes (a value of 0 indicates the color black) and this is followed by the ellipse() function to actually draw the circle. In this example the fill() function must be placed before the ellipse() function, or else the fill color will not be set properly. Statement order also affects how shapes are rendered when they overlap; for example a shape that overlaps an existing shape (i.e. its drawing instructions come after those of the existing shape) will appear "on top of" it. As a result the portion of the existing shape that overlaps the new shape will be blocked out, unless the new shape is opaque (i.e., its opacity is set with the fill() function).

Programming Approaches
There are three approaches available for programming with Processing: 1) Basic, 2) Continuous, and 3) Java. The **Basic** mode is used to perform tasks or draw static images without any animation or user interaction. The **Continuous** mode enables user interaction via keyboard and mouse events, and the creation of animations. You enable the continuous mode by implementing the setup() and draw() functions; setup() is executed once when the program starts, and draw() is executed repeatedly at the rate you specify with the frameRate() function. The **Java** mode enables you to write complete Java programs to be written from within the Processing environment.

Language and APIs
Processing contains a core set of language elements installed in the development environment that are directly available for creating sketches. The APIs are grouped into the following categories:

- **Structure** – common language structural elements, reserved keywords, general-purpose operators and functions.
- **Environment** – functions for managing the Processing operating environment.
- **Data** – reserve words and classes for specifying data types, and functions for manipulating data.
- **Control** – language elements for flow control, looping, and relational logic.

- **Shape** – classes and functions for the creation, manipulation, and control of (2D, 3D) drawing shapes.
- **Input** – classes and functions that support input data processing, whether from an input device (keyboard, mouse), file, or the internet, and provide time of day/year data.
- **Output** – functions that render data (text, images) to the display window or a file.
- **Transform** – functions that provide the abilities to perform coordinate system rotations and transformations. Performing a coordinate system rotation or transformation effectively changes its viewpoint; i.e. what the rendered image looks like.
- **Lights, Camera** – functions that enable you to manipulate lighting effects, viewpoints and projects, coordinates, and material properties for 3D rendering.
- **Color** – functions for setting the color and transparency of shapes.
- **Image** – classes and functions that enable you to load, display, and manipulate images.
- **Rendering** – classes and functions that provide access to the graphics and rendering contexts for drawing to an off-screen buffer or configuring a graphics renderer.
- **Typography** – classes and functions for rendering typography in a sketch (e.g., font management, etc.).
- **Math** – classes and functions for performing mathematical operations.
- **Constants** – constant values (PI, TWO_PI, HALF_PI, QUARTER_PI).

The Processing APIs are fully documented at http://processing.org/reference/.

Libraries

The Processing environment contains numerous software libraries for creating and editing computer graphics. These can be categorized as follows:

Imported Libraries

The imported libraries are included with the Processing environment but must be imported into a sketch via the **Import Library ...** command in the Sketch menu. A complete list is documented at the Processing website under libraries (http://processing.org/reference/libraries/).

Contributed Libraries

These libraries must be downloaded separately and placed within the *libraries* folder of the Processing environment sketchbook. The sketchbook location can be found in the Preferences window via the **Preferences** command in the File menu. Contributed libraries are developed and maintained by members of the Processing community. More information is provided at the Processing website under libraries.

Downloading and Installing Processing

The Processing development environment can be downloaded from the Processing website (http://processing.org/dowload). Processing is available for Mac, Windows, and Linux-based computers. The Processing *Getting Started* web page (http://processing.org/learning/gettingstarted/) contains instructions for installing the program; here's a brief summary of the installation steps for each supported platform:

- The *Mac OS X* version is packaged in a .zip file. Double-click this file to extract the Processing program and its icon will be displayed.

  You can double-click this icon to start the program.
- The *Windows* version is packaged in a .zip file. Double-click the zip file to locate the program in the zip folder. Drag the program (processing.exe) to a location on your hard drive. You can now double-click the processing application (processing.exe) icon to start the program.
- The instructions for installing the program on *Linux* are included at the Getting Started web page.

First Sketch – Graphics and Animation

All right, now you're ready to begin creating graphics. The one we create in this first sketch will look like this

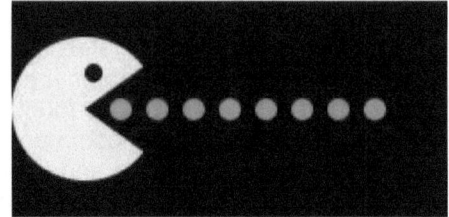

Figure 50. Pac-Man Graphic Image

As you can see, this is a simple graphic of the classic video game Pac-Man and his favorite food (Pac-dots). We'll begin by creating the graphics for this scene and then animate it to show Pac-Man eating the Pac-dots.

Start the Processing IDE
First start Processing as explained previously; the Processing text editor will be displayed

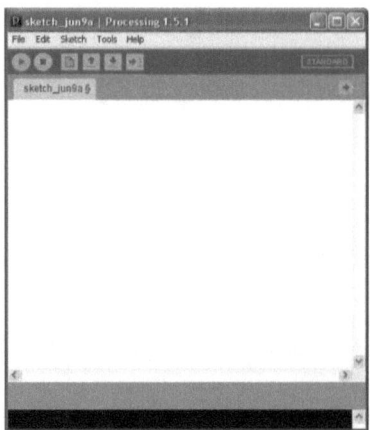

Figure 51. Processing Text Editor

As shown in the Figure the text editor window includes a Toolbar with several buttons, tabs, the text editor canvas, a message area, and a console.

The **Run** button runs your program and displays its output in the Processing Sketch window. The **Stop** button stops program execution. The **New** button creates a new sketch. The **Open** button opens the specified program file. The **Save** button saves your program in the folder you specify. The **Export Applet** button exports your program in a format that can be run from a browser. Note that the Processing menu (located above the main window) includes other commands in addition to those mentioned here.

Creating the Graphics

Now let's create the graphics, we'll start with Pac-Man and then create the Pac-dots. The first thing we'll do is create the sketch window using the `size()` function. In the text editor window type enter the following code

```
size(240, 120);
```

This creates a grid 240 pixels wide by 120 pixels high (Note that Processing programming statements (i.e. instructions) are terminated with a semicolon). Now let's save (using the **Save** button) and then run (using the **Run** button) our program to verify that we have the expected output. The Processing sketch window should display as follows

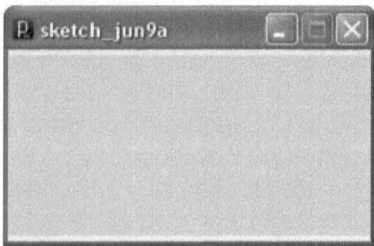

Figure 52. Processing Display Window

Great, so far so good, we have created our sketch window with the size specified. Now let's change the grid background so that it's black, we can do this with the `background()` function. On the next line in the editor window add the following code.

```
background(0);
```

This function sets the color used for the background of the sketch window; a single integer argument provided for the function is used to specify a grayscale setting ranging from white (value = 255) to black (value = 0). If you run the sketch again (don't forget to save it first!) the sketch window should now be black. OK, next let's add Pac-Man to the sketch; looking at the original figure we can see that the Pac-Man graphic is composed of a circular head (with an arc cutout) and an eye.

Let's start with Pac-Man's head. The `arc()` function can be used to draw an arc; in the editor window add the following code.

```
noStroke();
fill(234,247,40);
arc(40, 60, 80, 80, PI/5, TWO_PI-PI/5);
```

Let's talk about this code for a few moments. The `noStroke()` function disables drawing an outline around any subsequent shape(s). The `fill()` function sets the color used for any subsequent shape(s) drawn. The three arguments to the function (234, 247, 40) are the RGB values to create the color yellow for our Pac-Man shape. It can be pretty difficult to figure out the correct RGB values to create the color you want, so Processing includes a color selector tool (in the **Tools** menu above) that can be used to get the RGB values for the desired color. Finally the `arc()` function actually draws the arc shape; the values of its arguments are defined as (in order): x-coordinate (in the display window), y-coordinate, arc width, arc height (both in pixels), angle to start the arc, angle to end the arc. Note that an arc's angles are specified in radians. So, the code above specifies an arc located at coordinates (40, 60) on the display window, with a width and height of 80 pixels, which begins at `PI/5` radians (32 degrees) and ends at `TWO_PI-PI/5` radians (328 degrees). OK, now you may be wondering, what are radians and what are PI and `TWO_PI`? Well, PI represents the mathematical constant *pi*, whose value is (approximately) 3.14159 radians; in degrees this equals 180. So `PI/5` equals 32 degrees and `TWO_PI-PI/5` equals 328 degrees. If you save and run the program now you should see Pac-Man displayed against a black background; now let's add his eye.

The `ellipse()` function can be used to draw his eye; we want it to be drawn on his head a little to the right and slightly up (with respect to the center). In the editor window add the following code.

```
fill(0);
ellipse(45, 40, 10, 10);
```

This draws his eye, a black 10x10 pixel circle at coordinates (45, 40) on the display window. So far the program should look like this

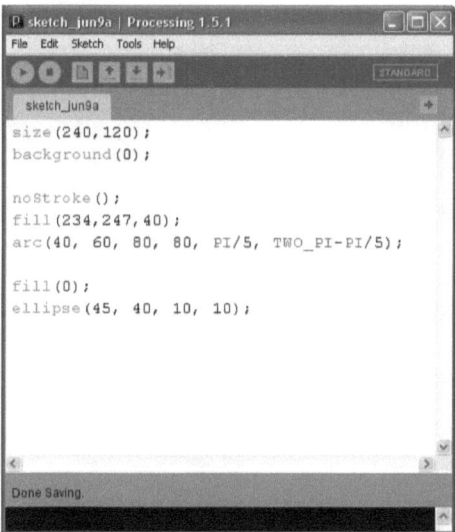

Figure 53. Code for Pac-Man Graphics

Notice that I added a few blank lines to improve clarity. If you save and run the program now you should see (in the display window)

Figure 54. Pac-Man Display

Perfect! We've completed the graphic for Pac-Man; now let's add the Pac-dots.

The Pac-dots are just one row of small circles that begin right after Pac-Man's mouth. I've updated the program for this below and also added some comment lines (the lines beginning with //); look it over for a minute and then we'll discuss it.

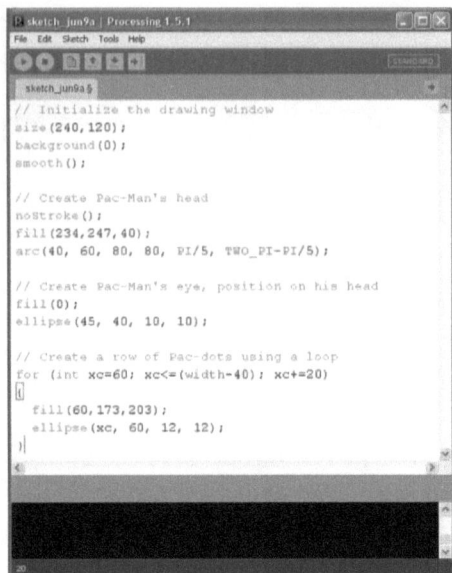

Figure 55. Code for Pac-Man and Pac-dots Graphics

You can see that the `fill()` and `ellipse()` functions are used to create the Pac-dots, but what's this other code doing; specifically the line beginning with `for`. That line of code marks the beginning of a `for` loop; this enables the same code to be executed repeatedly. The code within a `for` loop runs until a condition defined by the corresponding `for` statement is no longer `true`. The syntax of a `for` loop is

```
for (initialization; exit condition; incrementor)
{
  code
}
```

The `for` statement at the beginning of the loop includes an *initialization* statement, an *exit condition*, and an *incrementor*. The initialization code performs any initialization (of variables, etc.) required for the code that executes within the body of the loop (the *code* between the braces). Each time the loop starts, the exit condition is checked; if it evaluates to `true`, the code within the loop is executed. The incrementor code is typically used to increment (or decrement) one or more variables that are checked by the exit condition; hence it controls when you exit the loop. Once the exit condition evaluates to `false`, the loop is exited and the code that follows the `for` loop is executed.

What this all means is that the loop we have programmed will draw Pac-dots in a row across the window at a constant y-coordinate of 40 pixels, starting at x-coordinate 60, and spaced by 20 pixels, until we reach an x-coordinate of 200. In other words, the Pac-dots will be drawn at coordinates (60, 60), (80, 60), (100, 60), (120, 60), (140, 60), (160, 60), (180, 60), and (200, 60). Once you get the hang of it, you'll see that loops are very useful programming constructs.

Besides the comment lines, there is one other line of code that I added, can you find it? If you answered the line with the `smooth()` function, you're correct. This function removes the graininess of your graphics, drawing them with smooth edges. If you don't mind the jagged edges that can be apparent with digital images, you don't have to include this statement; it's your choice.

If you save and run the program now you should see (in the display window).

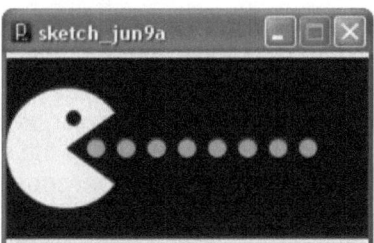

Figure 56. Pac-Man and Pac-dots Display

Great, we have completed our Pac-Man graphics; now let's turn this into an animation!

Animating the Graphics
In order to animate this sketch to show Pac-Man consuming the Pac-dots, we need to understand how Processing performs animation. An animated sketch is drawn as a series of frames, each of which is slightly different from the previous. To create the illusion of movement the images are sequentially displayed on the computer screen at a rate which gives the illusion of motion. With that in mind, Processing provides the built-in functions `setup()` and `draw()` to support animation according

to this method. If your sketch includes the `setup()` function it is called once, at the beginning of program execution; within the body of this function you include the initialization code for your program. If you include the `draw()` function it will be called repeatedly; it is within this function body that you include the code for drawing your animation frames. You specify the rate at which frames are displayed with the `frameRate()` function, where the value in parenthesis is the number of frames to draw per second (fps). The frame rate would typically be set during initialization, for example the following `setup()` function code will create a 300x300 pixel sketch window with a frame rate of 25 fps.

```
void setup()
{
  size(300, 300);
  frameRate(25);
}
```

As mentioned above, animation works by displaying an image on the screen and repeatedly replacing it with a new image that is similar, but advanced slightly in time. Hence each time the `draw()` function runs it should create a frame advanced in time from the previous one. When creating the animation on top of a background that is updated continuously (as is the case here where consumed Pac-dots should no longer be displayed) it is recommended to update only the portion of the scene that changes, and not completely draw a new scene for each frame. This can be done by erasing the Pac-Man object drawn in the previous frame prior to drawing the object for the current frame. In addition, the entire animation will execute in a loop that repeats when Pac-Man has consumed all the Pac-dots and reached the right edge of the display.

We'll now look at an updated version of the program that animates Pac-Man to show him eating the Pac-dots. The program is still in one sketch, but as it is much longer than the previous version it is displayed below in three separate figures. Look over this code and update your program accordingly, and then we'll discuss it.

Figure 57. Pac-Man Sketch, setup() and draw() Functions

The sketch now begins with an initialization section where we initialize variables that will be used throughout program execution. Next we implement the `setup()` and `draw()` functions; the `setup()` function creates a 240x120 pixel drawing window with a black background, sets up the renderer for smooth images, turns off shape outlines, and sets the frame rate to 25 fps. There is one other statement in the body of the `setup()` function – immediately before the `frameRate()` function we call the `drawPacDots()` function; this is a function we have written ourselves to draw the Pac-dots in the scene. The code for this function is further down in the scene and we'll talk about it shortly. The `draw()` function is called every frame and thus performs the animation. It checks to see if the scene should be initialized; if so a full complement of Pac-dots is drawn in the scene. It then executes the `createPacManDrawingFrame()` function. This is another function we have written to draw the frames for the animation. In your program this code should immediately follow the `draw()` function and is shown in the following figure.

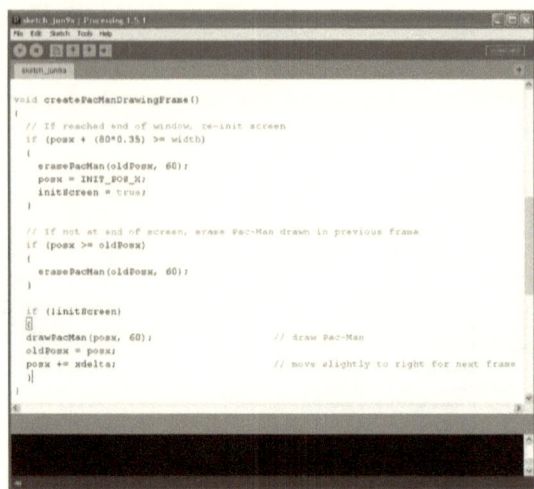

Figure 58. Pac-Man Sketch, Create Animation Frame

The `createPacManDrawingFrame()` function includes plenty of comments to clarify the programming logic. We want the animation to show Pac-Man moving across the screen, gobbling up Pac-dots as he goes. To do this, the program logic first computes how far to the right Pac-Man has moved (this value is stored in the variable `posx`). The actual width of the window is stored in the variable `width`. If Pac-Man has reached close to the right edge of the window, then his position is reset to the starting point and the screen will be initialized in the next frame. If Pac-Man has not reached the edge of the screen, then the Pac-Man image from the previous frame is erased. Finally Pac-Man is drawn and his position is advanced to the right for the next frame. There are two additional functions that we created to draw and erase Pac-Man; this code is shown below.

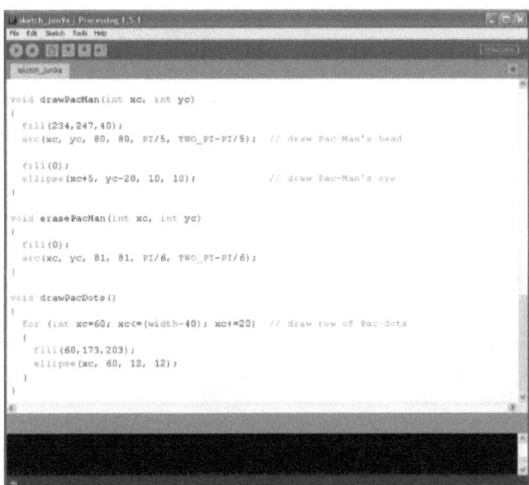

Figure 59. Pac-Man Sketch, Drawing Functions

The drawPacMan() and erasePacMan() functions have code that we wrote earlier when creating the Pac-Man graphics, however now variables are used for Pac-Man's position on the screen so that we can create animation frames. Also the code for the drawPacDots() function is shown; this is identical to the code we wrote earlier to draw the Pac-dots.

If you save and run the program now you should see in the display window Pac-Man gobbling up the Pac-dots; once he reaches the end of the window the animation begins again with a new set of dots for Pac-Man to consume. You can close the window at any time (or hit the **Stop** button) to stop the animation. Great job, you have just created your first computer animation!

Second Sketch – OpenGL 3D Images

OK, now that we have some computer graphics programming experience, let's create a 3D graphic that will be rendered using the OpenGL renderer. The graphic is shown below.

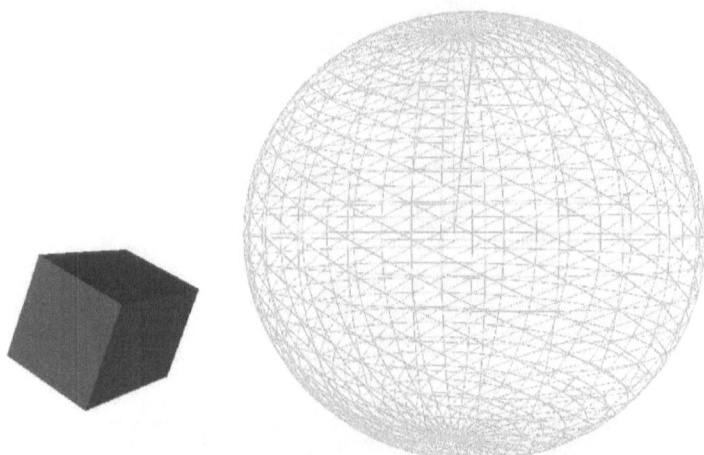

Figure 60. Processing 3D Image Rendered with OpenGL

It's a simple rendering of a 3D cube approaching a large sphere. Note that the two view objects have different perspectives, this illustration a few of the features of 3D graphics. Here's the code for the 3D image; first look it over (of course create a new sketch and type it in yourself if you wish!) and then we'll discuss it.

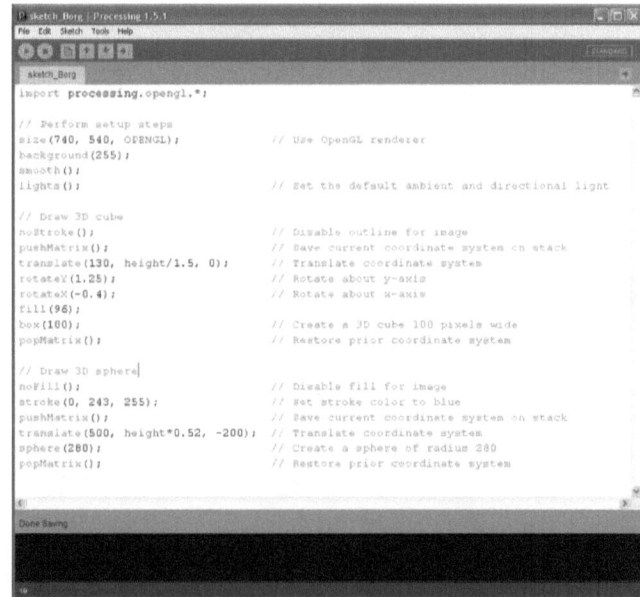

Figure 61. 3D OpenGL Image Code

The first line we see is an **import** statement; specifically it imports the OpenGL library so that it can be used within the sketch. This code doesn't have to be entered directly; you can import a library by using the **Import Library ...** command in the Sketch menu.

The next four lines of code setup the display window, notice that the `size()` function includes the argument `OPENGL`; this causes Processing to use OpenGL for rendering the sketch. The `lights()` function sets the values for lighting when performing 3D rendering.

The next 8 lines of code draw the 3D cube; the comments provide a good description of what the code does, but let's talk a little bit about what the `pushMatrix()` and `popMatrix()` functions do. Earlier in this section we talked about coordinate systems; in geometry coordinate systems are used to uniquely determine a location in space. Processing utilizes Cartesian coordinates; hence three numbers - its x, y, and z-coordinates, identify each point in three-dimensional space.

A matrix, a rectangular array of numbers, can represent the orientation of a coordinate system. A transformation (i.e. translation or rotation) of this matrix, from the viewer's perspective, is the same thing as a transformation of the object being viewed. A simple example would be looking at a 3D object from its front, top, and side; each has a different viewpoint.

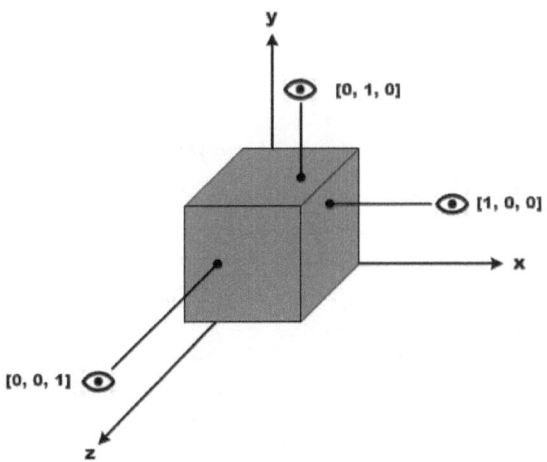

Figure 62. Example Viewpoints for a 3D Cube

The viewpoint directly facing the x-y plane is perpendicular to a point in space with the [0, 0, 1] coordinates; comparable points ([1, 0, 0], [0, 1, 0]) are perpendicular to the y-z and x-z planes. The `pushMatrix()` and `popMatrix()` functions enable you to save and retrieve a coordinate system, and hence a viewpoint. Typically you would save the current viewpoint (using `pushMatrix()`), perform one or more transformations (translations, rotations, scaling, etc.) and draw an object at this perspective, then return to the previous viewpoint (using `popMatrix()`). This could be done for any number of objects in the scene, enabling you to have fine-grain control of 3D objects in space.

OK, returning to the code, you see that first the code saves the current coordinate system (using the `pushMatrix()` function). Then it transforms the coordinate system by including arguments that translate and scale it in size. Next it rotates the coordinate system about both the y and x axes. Finally the cube is drawn in the new coordinate system and the original coordinate system is restored. As shown in the figure, the rendered cube has a perspective that reflects these transformations.

The last 6 lines of code draw the 3D sphere; this code is very similar to that written above, but in this case we are using the `sphere()` function to draw the sphere. Again we use the `pushMatrix()` and `popMatrix()` functions to surround the transformations and then return us to the original viewpoint. As the `noFill()` function is executed prior to drawing the sphere, only its outline is displayed.

Processing Key Features

To summarize, the key features of the Processing Development Environment (PDE) are:

- Processing IDE – tool for developing, running, and distributing Processing programs. It includes a text editor, a display window, and an assortment of PDE commands.
- Processing Language – the core language and APIs used for developing Processing programs.
- Processing Libraries – a collection of imported and contributed libraries that extend the capabilities of the platform.

You now have a good introduction to Processing and how you can use it to create and edit computer graphics. Processing has been designed to be easy to use and I hope that you gained that impression by working through these examples. This code is all open source so feel free to modify the examples presented here as you please, also check out the Processing website (http://processing.org/) for more information, user forums, etc.

Summary

Congratulations, this has been our longest chapter to date and you've done a great job absorbing this material. Computer graphics is a vast field, and advances in this area will continue to be made as the technologies (both software and hardware) evolve. In this chapter we learned about the basics of computer digital imaging and animation, along with image modeling and rendering. We then looked at several representative languages and software libraries that can be used to create computer graphics, and create a couple of graphics ourselves. With this introduction you now have a good foundation to begin programming your own computer graphics, sweet! Now you may be thinking, "Programming graphics was a lot of fun, how can we top this"? Well, here's a hint – do you like video games? So when you're ready turn the page and let's learn how to do some game programming!

Chapter **12**
Game Programming

Let's admit it - we enjoy playing video games, and each of us has our favorites. Some of us are old-school and enjoy playing the classics like Pac-Man and Space Invaders, while others may be into the latest multiplayer online games. There's no doubt that video gaming is extremely popular, especially on mobile devices, where they are by far the most commonly downloaded apps. So a great way to top off everything we have done thus far is with game programming. Now developing a game is a lot of fun but is by no means easy. In the early days of video gaming, a single programmer could develop a game. Nowadays a team of over 100 people may be involved in the development of a sophisticated game that includes custom, life-like 3D graphics and animations, enhanced sound effects, and a host of other features. The aim of this chapter is to provide you with a solid introduction to game programming by focusing on its key concepts. We'll start with an overview of game development and the different styles of games, next learn the basic structure of game programs, briefly review a few of the many game development platforms and software libraries available today, and finally examine code for a simple game that you can download and try out yourself!

Introduction

The first video games were developed in the 1950s; one of the earliest was a version of Tic-Tac-Toe that ran on an EDSAC mainframe computer. In fact, the majority of early video games was developed at universities and ran on mainframes. In the 1960s video games began to be distributed with computer systems and traded over the Internet, and the first video gaming consoles were developed. Commercial arcade video games and game consoles began to be produced in the 1970s, and in the late 1970s commercial computer-based video games began to be developed. Due to technology limitations these early games had limited graphics and content. However, as computers continued to become more powerful and the computer gaming industry grew, more sophisticated games were produced. By the late 1980s, video game consoles (in particular the Nintendo Entertainment System) lead to many advances in game development. The 1990s saw the rise in PC-based gaming, the initial appearance of mobile gaming, and advances in 3D graphics technology. By this time, game development often required a team of developers and significant capital investment. From the 2000s on, aided by advances in computer processing capability, the explosion of mobile devices, and the availability of game development software, the gaming industry has continued to expand. With the resources at our disposal, it is now possible for just about anyone (and that includes you!) to develop a video game.

Game Genres

Video games are played on a multitude of platforms, and distributed through numerous channels. With few exceptions, most games can be categorized into one or more of several popular game styles, or *genres*. Each genre has general characteristics that distinguish it, and emphasizes key functional elements that play a major role during game development. This section provides an overview of these genres.

Action

Action games feature real-time player interactions that emphasize physical tests of skill, and typically require quick reflexes and careful timing to complete challenges. Usually the player controls a character or a weapon, and must perform actions like collecting objects, avoiding objects, and battling enemies, or avoiding enemies altogether. Common types of action games include fighting games, shooter games, stealth games, and jumping (i.e. platform) games. Key action game elements include real-time animation, user interaction, and game physics.

Adventure
Adventure games focus on storytelling, and usually feature exploration, puzzle solving, and collecting items. They typically draw on other media such as literature and film for the plot line that unfolds, and feature little or no action. They are in almost all cases designed for a single player and feature turn-based game play. Key adventure game elements include computer graphics, animation, and game play.

Action-Adventure
An action-adventure game combines elements of both the adventure and action game genres. They typically feature problem-solving and physical challenges. The key action-adventure game elements combine those listed for those genres.

Role-Playing
In role-playing games the player controls one or a small group of characters and lives as this character(s) in a fictional world. Typically the characters improve as they progress through the game (win battles, succeed in challenges) and the games have a strong story line, often with a fantasy, sci-fi, or real world setting. Role-playing games typically emphasize computer graphics, animation, game physics, and game play.

Simulation
Simulation games attempt to replicate real-world experiences. The simulation follows real-world rules as much as possible, and the players employ their understanding of these rules when confronted with situations in the game. The game play may be real-time or turn-based, and may feature multiple players. Common categories of simulation games include vehicle, process (construction and management), life, and sports. Key simulation game elements include real-time animation, (multi) user interaction, graphics, and game physics.

Strategy
Strategy games typically have a player managing a limited set of resources to achieve a specific goal. Strategy games can be turn-based or real-time, and many of those currently being produced feature military battles involving combative play and

competition. Key strategy game elements include real-time animation, user interaction, and game physics.

Casual

Casual games are those commonly played by casual gamers; they tend to be short, without a story line, and are geared towards relaxation. These games are typically turn-based, use less computing resources, and hence can be easily played on mobile devices. Common categories include puzzle games, card games, board games, casino games, and word games. Key casual game elements include user interaction and game play.

Massively Multiplayer Online

Massively multiplayer online (MMO) games may feature thousands of simultaneous players. These games basically add the capability for online gaming to the genres specified above. Hence they add multi-user interaction and networking to the list of key elements for developing MMO games.

Functional Components

In the preceding section we discussed common game genres and specified some key functional elements that factor into game programming. Now we want to better understand each of these elements and the functionality they provide. To do that, let's review the major components of a video game.

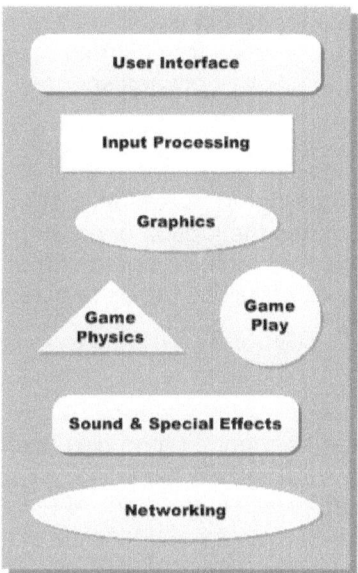

Figure 63. Game Program Functional Components

User Interface
The user interface code implements the game input and output functionality. The input controls allow the player to control the game; they may be game-specific (control knobs, joystick, etc.), utilize standard input devices (e.g., keyboard, mouse, etc.), or some combination of the above. The output functionality displays relevant game information (current score, level, etc.), updating it in real-time as the game progresses. The user interface also implements accessory screens that enable the player to configure the game or obtain useful information (e.g. help screens, etc.).

Input Processing
The input processing functionality receives inputs from all available data sources and invokes the appropriate components to process this data accordingly. Common input data sources include the user interface (e.g., mouse, keyboard, and touchscreen data) and sensors (e.g., mobile device gyroscope, accelerometer, and/or compass data).

Graphics & Animation
This code supports the display of computer graphics and animation. This includes the management of graphics for

efficient and accurate rendering using the appropriate graphics libraries, creation of animation frames, and the management of game scenes and transitions between scenes.

Game Physics

The game physics functionality incorporates physics into the game *virtual world*, in order to make these effects seem real to the player. This includes the motion of game players and objects due to inputs, the general motion of game objects over time as a result of physical laws, collisions between objects (both moving and stationary), etc.

Game Play & AI

The game play and Artificial Intelligence (AI) components are designed to direct and enhance game play, executing game functionality and interacting with the player(s) according to the game rules and strategies. In particular AI techniques are commonly used to simulate the appearance of intelligence in the behavior of *non-playable characters* (NPCs). Examples of these effects include increasing game difficulty levels, complex and varied NPC movements, and evolving, different NPC personalities.

Sound & Special Effects

The sound and special effects functionality plays background music and targeted game sounds, and performs special visual effects (particle effects, etc.) designed to enhance game play.

Communication & Networking

The communications and networking code enables game and player interaction with external systems and/or other players, commonly over a network such as the Internet.

Game Structure

One of the factors that differentiate game programming from other types of computer programming is the continuous nature of video games. Specifically, many games are designed such that the game environment (i.e. *game world*) is continuously updated (i.e. animated), and also responds to inputs in real-time. The animation is performed by the sequential display of images, each of which is (typically) slightly different from the previous one, at a rate that gives the illusion of motion. The inputs can be received from both the player (via input devices) and input sensors.

Game programs are commonly designed with a *game loop* to implement this continuous, real-time behavior.

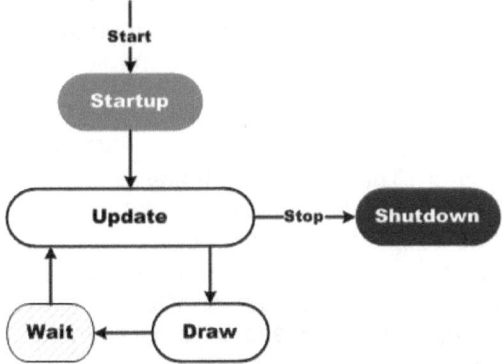

Figure 64. Frame Rate Limited Game Loop

During game **startup** the program is initialized. The **update** stage of the loop receives inputs and updates the game state appropriately. The game state updates typically involve updating the game 'virtual world' per the game physics and game play components. The **draw** stage renders the updated game scene (i.e. its graphics, sound, and special effects) to the output device(s). The **wait** stage is then entered if there is time left over before starting the loop again. The game loop continues until the game ends or the player stops the game.

Game Development Platforms
Game programming can be a significant undertaking and requires a broad understanding of many disciplines (graphics, animation, physics, AI, computer performance and resource management, input/output processing, etc.). Often there are numerous types of functionality that must be implemented; in addition the game must also be fun and easy to play. If any of its key functional elements or the user experience is unsatisfactory then the game will not be successful.

The availability of specialized game programming libraries and platforms greatly facilitates game development. They are offered for multiple programming languages, and can be used to develop games that will be deployed on numerous targets (computers, devices, etc.). These tools provide a wealth of commonly used game functionality (game physics engine, AI software, etc.), thus enabling the programmer to reuse the code provided by these libraries and focus his/her programming efforts on code that is specific to the game itself. The following paragraphs provide a brief overview of several game programming libraries and platforms in use today; the **References** Appendix documents more information on specific game programming resources.

Unity

Unity is a multi-platform tool set for creating 3D video games and interactive content. The development environment tools run on the Microsoft Windows and Apple OS X platforms, and can be used to develop games that run on multiple platforms (computers, game consoles, and devices, even online in browsers). The tool set consists of an IDE for developing game program code (using the C++ and C# programming languages) and a game engine for game execution.

Gamestudio

Gamestudio is a game development system used to create 3D games and virtual reality applications. Gamestudio is specifically designed for programmers of various skill levels, making it a good game development system for hobbyists, artists, as well as experienced programmers. The development environment tools include an IDE and game engine and run on Microsoft Windows; both free and commercial versions are available.

Cocos2d

Cocos2d is a free, open-source framework for building 2D games and graphical/interactive applications. It is a flexible, feature-filled framework that is designed to make game programming simpler. Versions have been developed for a variety of languages and platforms, including Mac OS X, iOS devices, Android devices, and even browsers. Cocos2d has become one of the most popular 2D game engines for the iOS platform and it has even been used to develop commercial games such as the iOS version of Farmville. Extensions to the platform include Cocos3d, which adds 3D game and application development capabilities.

Developing a Kobold2D Game

There's no better way to complete this introduction to game programming than by getting some hands-on experience. This means examining some code for a simple game; the game we'll use for this was developed with the **Kobold2D** platform. We'll start off with a brief overview of Kobold2D and identify its main features. Next we'll download and install the software. Finally we'll look at download and examine an example game that can be used as reference for developing your own games.

Kobold2D Overview

Kobold2D is an extended version of the Cocos2d framework. Specifically it augments this framework with additional tools, developer resources, and other software libraries that make for more efficient and productive game development. Kobold2D is designed for developing Mac OS X and iOS games; its minimum hardware and software requirements are an Intel-based Mac computer running Mac OS X 10.6 or later. An iOS device is also required if developing games targeted for these devices. The Xcode IDE and Objective-C language are used for programming with Kobold2D.

Features

The main features of Kobold2D include the software libraries, the installer, documentation, project templates, and the provided example games. These features make it easy to quickly begin developing games.

Software Libraries

The Kobold2D software libraries provide a complete set of functionality for game development. Here's a brief overview of these libraries:

- **Kobold2D** - the Kobold2D library consists of a set of classes and files, along with extensions to existing Cocos2d classes.
- **Cocos2d-iPhone** - all of the Cocos2d software libraries are provided with Kobold2D.
- **Cocos3d** - cocos3d is an extension to Cocos2d that adds capabilities (specifically 3D graphics) for building 3D games and interactive applications.
- **Lua** - Lua support for Kobold2D is provided with the Lua software library. Lua is an *embedded* programming language (i.e. Lua program statements are embedded within another program). It is used to create text files that contain the startup configuration settings for Kobold2D games.
- **Audio** - Kobold2D includes two audio libraries for games, ObjectAL and CocosDenshion. CocosDenshion

can be used for both Mac OS X and iOS games, while ObjectAL works for iOS games only.

- **Physics Engines** - Kobold2D includes three game physics libraries: Chipmunk, Chipmunk Space Manager, and Box2D. Box2D is written in C++; in addition it has a few features not available with the Chipmunk engines. Chipmunk is written in C while Chipmunk Space Manager adds an Objective-C object-oriented interface to Chipmunk.
- **iSimulate** - iSimulate is a library that adds multi-touch, accelerometer, GPS, and compass events to the iOS simulator.
- **SneakyInput** - SneakyInput is a library that consists of a collection of game controls (joystick, joypad, input buttons).
- **Utilities** - Kobold2D contains several libraries that perform various utility functions.

Installer

Kobold2D provides tools for installing the software in the Xcode IDE. It also includes a tool for upgrading a Kobold2D project to a newer version and upgrading existing Cocos2d games to Kobold2D.

Documentation

Kobold2D provides a collection of documentation that includes reference manuals (Programming Guide, User's Guide, etc.), FAQs, and APIs for all of its libraries. The libraries are available online, or can be downloaded for offline viewing.

Template Projects

Each Kobold2D game is developed within Xcode as an Xcode project. Kobold2D includes numerous template projects that can be used to learn about specific features or as a starting point for creating new games. Examples include a basic template, a template that shows you how to create particle effects, a template for creating 3D games, templates for using the provide physics engines, templates for working with tilemaps, and a template for working with texture atlases.

Example Games

Kobold2D includes several example games, each of which is packaged in its own Xcode project. These games are fully playable, and provide working examples that you can learn from and/or use as a foundation for developing your own games.

Install the Software

Now that we have completed our overview of Kobold2D we can begin working with an actual game! The first step is to download and install Kobold2D; instructions are provided at the Kobold2D website (http://www.kobold2d.com). The example game is a version of tic-tac-toe; you can download it at http://www.motupresse.com/p4e/code/iTicTacToe.zip. The game was developed on a Mac computer running Mac OS X 10.8 (Mountain Lion), iOS 6, Xcode 4.5, and using the current version of Kobold2D (v2.0.3). If you have a compatible Mac computer you can install the software, or just follow along in the subsequent paragraphs.

The game is designed to run on iOS (iPhone, iPad, iPod Touch) devices; an iPad version is shown below.

Figure 65. iPad Tic-Tac-Toe Game

This example illustrates several key components of video games and game design. The game is for a single player and works as follows – the player makes a move by touching within the desired square, thereby marking an **X** on the board. The computer then makes a move, marking an **O** in an unoccupied square. Play continues on, alternating between player moves and computer moves, until either the player/computer gets tic-tac-toe or all moves have been played without a winner (a *draw*). To start another game the player touches the appropriate button –

touching the **Player Starts** button enables the player to make the first move, while touching the **Computer Starts** button results in the computer making the first move. The game also displays win/loss/draw status, and includes sound effects.

Game Design

Even for a simple game like this, there is a considerable amount of functionality implemented here, particularly in the areas of game play, graphics, the user interface, input processing, and sound effects. Object-Oriented software design principles were used to develop the software in an organized, modular manner. A brief description of the game's key classes follows:

- GameScene

  The GameScene class organizes and manages the scenario, or setting, for the game. The principal elements of the game scene are the game board and the user interface. As such the GameScene class is responsible for creating these elements and providing access to them as needed.
- UILayer

  The UILayer class creates the user interface for the game. The UI consists of a menu used to initiate game play, a title label, and a status label that displays win/loss/draw status.
- GameLayer

  The GameLayer class implements the tic-tac-toe game board. It uses graphics routines to draw the board, and input processing logic to respond to touch input and mark the game board squares appropriately.
- GamePlayAI

  The GamePlayAI class provides game play logic; specifically it performs (computer) moves using a game theory algorithm, and determines when tic-tac-toe or a draw occurs.
- PlayingSquare

  The PlayingSquare class represents each square on the game board; it knows its position on the board and how to draw itself in response to player/computer input.

Open the Project

If you haven't already done so, download the iTicTacToe.zip file from http://www.motupresse.com/p4e/code. The file should then be unzipped into your Kobold2D projects directory (for Kobold2D version 2.0.3, the projects directory is named Kobold2D-2.0.3). Once completed you should see a `TicTacToe` folder in the Kobold2D projects directory; in that folder double-click the **TicTacToe.xcodeproj** file to start Xcode and open the project.

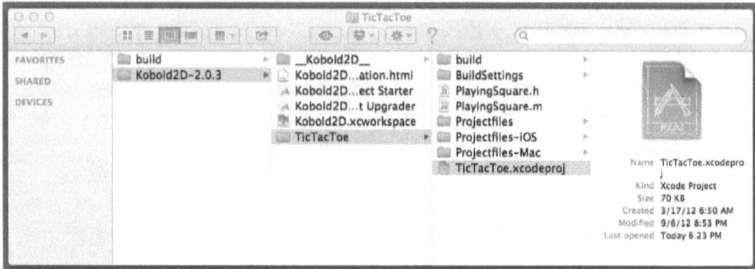

Figure 66. Starting the TicTacToe Project

The project includes numerous files and other project-specific resources. You can examine any file or resource by selecting it in the Project Navigator and viewing its contents in the Editor Window; in the figure below the `UILayer.m` file is displayed.

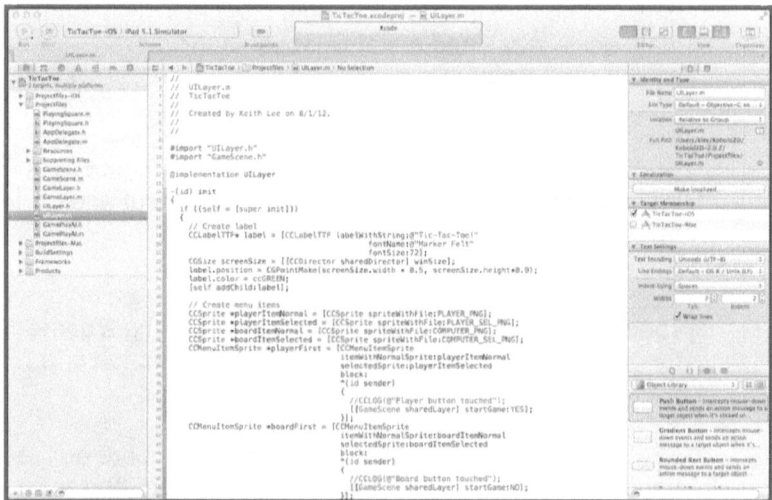

Figure 67. Xcode TicTacToe Project

Creating the Game Scene
The game scene user interface and game board are implemented with *layers* – specifically a game layer and a user

interface layer. Conceptually, in Kobold2D layers provide a mechanism for logically grouping game elements and also controlling how these elements are displayed in relation to each other. The game and user interface layers are added to the game scene in the GameScene class `init` method.

```
// Initialize the GameScene - add layers
-(id) init
{
  if ((self = [super init]))
  {
    NSAssert(gameSceneInstance == nil, @"another GameScene is already in use!");
    gameSceneInstance = self;

    // The GameLayer is where game play takes place, it contains the game board.
    GameLayer* gameLayer = [GameLayer node];
    [self addChild:gameLayer z:0 tag:LayerTagGameLayer];

    // The UserInterfaceLayer contains the controls and status messages
    UILayer* uiLayer = [UILayer node];
    [self addChild:uiLayer z:1 tag:LayerTagUILayer];
  }
  return self;
}
```

Figure 68. Game Scene - Add Layers

The user interface layer (files `UILayer.h`, `UILayer.m`) provides a menu with buttons for game control and displays labels that display a title and game status. The menu buttons respond to touch input, starting a new game with either the player or the computer making the first move. The following UILayer code (in file `UILayer.m`) creates the menu and the title label as described, positioning the title at the top of the screen and the menu at its bottom.

```
// Create label
CCLabelTTF* label = [CCLabelTTF labelWithString:@"Tic-Tac-Toe!"
                               fontName:@"Marker Felt"
                               fontSize:72];
CGSize screenSize = [[CCDirector sharedDirector] winSize];
label.position = CGPointMake(screenSize.width * 0.5, screenSize.height*0.9);
label.color = ccGREEN;
[self addChild:label];

// Create menu items
CCSprite *playerItemNormal = [CCSprite spriteWithFile:PLAYER_PNG];
CCSprite *playerItemSelected = [CCSprite spriteWithFile:PLAYER_SEL_PNG];
CCSprite *boardItemNormal = [CCSprite spriteWithFile:COMPUTER_PNG];
CCSprite *boardItemSelected = [CCSprite spriteWithFile:COMPUTER_SEL_PNG];
CCMenuItemSprite *playerFirst = [CCMenuItemSprite
                                 itemWithNormalSprite:playerItemNormal
                                 selectedSprite:playerItemSelected
                                 block:
                                 ^(id sender)
                                 {
                                     [[GameScene sharedLayer] startGame:YES];
                                 }];
CCMenuItemSprite *boardFirst = [CCMenuItemSprite
                                itemWithNormalSprite:boardItemNormal
                                selectedSprite:boardItemSelected
                                block:
                                ^(id sender)
                                {
                                    [[GameScene sharedLayer] startGame:NO];
                                }];

// Create menu
CCMenu *menu = [CCMenu menuWithItems:playerFirst, boardFirst, nil];
menu.position = CGPointMake(screenSize.width * 0.5, screenSize.height * 0.1);
[menu alignItemsHorizontallyWithPadding:20];
[self addChild:menu];
```

Figure 69. Create Menu and Label

Game Board Graphics

The game layer class (files GameLayer.h, GameLayer.m)
implements the game board, the 3x3 grid on which the tic-tac-toe
Xs and **Os** are displayed. There are a variety of approaches that
can be taken to draw the game board, for example displaying it
as a background texture or using graphics APIs. This program
uses graphics APIs, specifically the GameLayer class draw
method that is run during the game loop. The GameLayer
extends the cocos2d CCLayer class, which provides an empty
draw method. If a subclass of CCLayer (e.g. GameLayer)
overrides (i.e. implements) the draw method, this method will
then be executed by the Kobold2D (i.e. cocos2d) game engine at
the specified frame rate (for example, 30 times per second).

```
-(void)draw
{
    // Draw game board
    [self drawGameBoard];

    // If tic-tac-toe formed, draw winning line
    if ([gamePlayer getWinningSquares])
    {
        [self drawWinningLine];
    }
}
```

Figure 70. GameLayer draw Method

As shown in the above figure, the GameLayer `draw` method invokes the `drawGameBoard` method that renders the tic-tac-toe game board on the display.

```
// Draw tic-tac-toe 3x3 game board
-(void) drawGameBoard
{
    // Draw perimeter game box
    glEnable(GL_BLEND);
    glBlendFunc(GL_SRC_ALPHA, GL_ONE_MINUS_SRC_ALPHA);
    glLineWidth(4.0f);
    ccDrawColor4B(255, 255, 255, 255);
    ccDrawRect(gameLayerOrigin, gameLayerDest);

    // Then draw internal lines for each playing square
    // -- Vertical Line 1
    CGPoint vLine1Origin;
    CGPoint vLine1Dest;
    vLine1Origin.x = gameLayerOrigin.x + (gameLayerBox.size.width * 0.33);
    vLine1Origin.y = gameLayerOrigin.y;
    vLine1Dest.x = vLine1Origin.x;
    vLine1Dest.y = gameLayerOrigin.y + gameLayerBox.size.height;
    ccDrawLine(vLine1Origin, vLine1Dest);

    // -- Vertical Line 2
    CGPoint vLine2Origin;
    CGPoint vLine2Dest;
    vLine2Origin.x = gameLayerOrigin.x + (gameLayerBox.size.width * 0.66);
    vLine2Origin.y = gameLayerOrigin.y;
    vLine2Dest.x = vLine2Origin.x;
    vLine2Dest.y = gameLayerOrigin.y + gameLayerBox.size.height;
    ccDrawLine(vLine2Origin, vLine2Dest);

    // -- Horizontal Line 1
    CGPoint hLine1Origin;
    CGPoint hLine1Dest;
    hLine1Origin.x = gameLayerOrigin.x;
    hLine1Origin.y = gameLayerOrigin.y + (gameLayerBox.size.height * 0.66);
    hLine1Dest.x = hLine1Origin.x + gameLayerBox.size.width;
    hLine1Dest.y = hLine1Origin.y;
    ccDrawLine(hLine1Origin, hLine1Dest);

    // -- Horizontal Line 2
    CGPoint hLine2Origin;
    CGPoint hLine2Dest;
    hLine2Origin.x = gameLayerOrigin.x;
    hLine2Origin.y = gameLayerOrigin.y + (gameLayerBox.size.height * 0.33);
    hLine2Dest.x = hLine2Origin.x + gameLayerBox.size.width;
    hLine2Dest.y = hLine2Origin.y;
    ccDrawLine(hLine2Origin, hLine2Dest);
}
```

Figure 71. Game Board

Player Inputs

The game is designed to receive touch input so that the player can mark (unoccupied) squares on the game board. As such, the **GameLayer** `ccTouchBegan:withEvent:` method processes touch input.

```
// Handle touch inputs
-(BOOL) ccTouchBegan:(UITouch*)touch withEvent:(UIEvent *)event
{
    CGPoint location = [GameScene locationFromTouch:touch];
    bool isTouchHandled = [self isTouchForMe:location];
    if (isTouchHandled && !alreadyMarked)
    {
        alreadyMarked = YES;

        // Run Actions on GameLayer
        for (int jj=0; jj<BOARD_COLS; jj++)
        {
            for (int ii=0; ii<BOARD_ROWS; ii++)
            {
                if ([self isTouch:location withinSquare:[boxes[ii][jj] getPlayingSquare]])
                {
                    [boxes[ii][jj] markSquare:YES andSetVisible:YES];
                    [[SimpleAudioEngine sharedEngine] playEffect:PLAYER_MOVE_EFFECT];
                    [gamePlayer incrementMovesPlayed];

                    // Check if tic-tac-toe formed or all moves played
                    if ([gamePlayer isTicTacToe])
                    {
                        [self displayWinMessage:YES];
                        [self setIsTouchEnabled:NO];
                        soundId = [[SimpleAudioEngine sharedEngine]
                                   playEffect:PLAYER_WIN_EFFECT];
                        return isTouchHandled;
                    }
                    else if ([gamePlayer maxMovesPlayed])
                    {
                        [self displayDrawMessage];
                        [self setIsTouchEnabled:NO];
                        soundId = [[SimpleAudioEngine sharedEngine] playEffect:DRAW_EFFECT];
                        return isTouchHandled;
                    }

                    // Now make computer move (AI runs)
                    [self scheduleOnce:@selector(computerMove) delay:1.0];
                    isTouchHandled = YES;
                    break;
                }
            }
        }
    }

    return isTouchHandled;
}
```

Figure 72. Handling Touch Inputs

This method is called whenever touch input is received. It determines if the touch input was received within the perimeter of the game board and, if so, within which game square. As shown in the figure above (the circled items), the code accomplishes this by invoking the methods `isTouchForMe:` and `isTouch:withinSquare:`. These methods are shown below.

```
// Checks if the touch location was within the game board.
-(bool) isTouchForMe:(CGPoint)touchLocation
{
  if (CGRectContainsPoint(gameLayerBox, touchLocation))
  {
    return YES;
  }
  return NO;
}

// Checks if the touch location was within a playing square.
-(bool) isTouch:(CGPoint)location withinSquare:(CGRect)box
{
  if (CGRectContainsPoint(box, location))
  {
    return YES;
  }
  return NO;
}
```

Figure 73. Processing Game Board Touch Events

After the player's input is received the GameLayer class
executes the game play logic using the GameLayer
`computerMove` method.

```
-(void) computerMove
{
  [gamePlayer markSquare];
  [[SimpleAudioEngine sharedEngine] playEffect:CPU_MOVE_EFFECT];
  [gamePlayer incrementMovesPlayed];

  // Check if tic-tac-toe formed or all moves played
  if ([gamePlayer isTicTacToe])
  {
    [self displayWinMessage:NO];
    soundId = [[SimpleAudioEngine sharedEngine] playEffect:CPU_WIN_EFFECT];
  }
  else if ([gamePlayer maxMovesPlayed])
  {
    [self displayDrawMessage];
    soundId = [[SimpleAudioEngine sharedEngine] playEffect:DRAW_EFFECT];
  }
  alreadyMarked = NO;
}
```

Figure 74. Computer Move Logic

Game Play and AI

The GamePlayAI class performs the main game play logic;
specifically it performs computer moves and determines if tic-tac-
toe or a draw has occurred. The GamePlayAI `markSquare`
method marks an unoccupied square on the game board; each
square is an instance of the PlayingSquare class.

```
-(void) markSquare
{
  int bestValue = -30;
  int bestPositionX = 0;
  int bestPositionY = 0;

  for (int ii=0; ii<3; ii++)
  {
    for (int jj=0; jj<3; jj++)
    {
      if ([board[ii][jj] getSquareMark] == NONE)
      {
        [board[ii][jj] markSquare:NO andSetVisible:NO];
        int returnedValue = [self evaluatePosition];
        if (returnedValue >= bestValue)
        {
          bestValue = returnedValue;
          bestPositionX = ii;
          bestPositionY = jj;
        }
        [board[ii][jj] clearSquare];
      }
    }
  }
  [board[bestPositionX][bestPositionY] markSquare:NO andSetVisible:YES];

}
```

Figure 75. Mark Board Square

It uses a game theory algorithm that evaluates the board to determine the best square to mark based on the squares already marked the benefits of marking each of the available remaining unoccupied squares. This algorithm is shown below.

```
-(int) evaluatePosition
{
  if ([self getMarkValueForCpuMarks:3 andPlayerMarks:0])
  {
    return 30;
  }
  else if ([self getMarkValueForCpuMarks:0 andPlayerMarks:3])
  {
    return 30;
  }
  else if ([self isAPitfall])
  {
    return -30;
  }
  else
  {
    int cm2 = [self getMarkValueForCpuMarks:2 andPlayerMarks:0];
    int cm1 = [self getMarkValueForCpuMarks:1 andPlayerMarks:0];
    int pm2 = [self getMarkValueForCpuMarks:0 andPlayerMarks:2];
    int pm1 = [self getMarkValueForCpuMarks:0 andPlayerMarks:1];
    int value = (3 * cm2) + cm1 - ((3 * pm2) + pm1);
    return value;
  }
}
```

Figure 76. Tic-Tac-Toe MinMax Algorithm

Once the best square is determined, it is marked and displayed using the PlayingSquare markSquare:andSetVisible: method

```
- (void) markSquare:(BOOL) player andSetVisible:(BOOL) visible
{
  if (!isSelected)
  {
    if (player)
    {
      xSprite.visible = visible;
      mark = Player;
    }
    else
    {
      oSprite.visible = visible;
      mark = Computer;
    }
    isSelected = YES;
  }
  else
  {
    if (player)
    {
      xSprite.visible = visible;
      mark = NONE;
    }
    else
    {
      oSprite.visible = visible;
      mark = NONE;
    }
    isSelected = NO;
  }
}
```

Figure 77. Playing Square - Mark and Set Visible

Note that the PlayingSquare class contains the functionality associated with each board square; specifically it loads the image files used to mark each square, and renders the correct image according to whether the player or computer is marking the square.

Sounds and Special Effects
The game includes sound effects that are played when a move is made and when game status (i.e., win/lose/draw) is determined. A sound effect is played using the Kobold2D CocosDenshion audio library, invoked with the SimpleAudioEngine playEffect: method.

```
[[SimpleAudioEngine sharedEngine] playEffect:PLAYER_WIN_EFFECT];
```

Figure 78. Playing Sound Effects

Let's Play!
If your computer is configured appropriately and you have loaded all of the required software, you can run the game by clicking the **Run** button from the Xcode toolbar (make sure you set the iPad Simulator as your target device). After a few moments you

should see the game in the simulator. Now go ahead, try it out and see if you can get tic-tac-toe!

Summary

Wow, this chapter has been a lot to absorb!! As you can now appreciate, game programming is pretty challenging, but also very rewarding. There's nothing quite like the sense of accomplishment you get from creating and then playing your own video game. You now have a solid understanding of the basic concepts for game programming, and are ready to take the next steps and begin creating your own games. The tic-tac-toe game you have been working with provides a good starting point, so feel free to use and/or modify it as you please.

Chapter 13
Next Steps

Well, this has been quite a journey. We have been on a whirlwind tour and covered quite a few programming topics, so I would like to thank you for taking the time to read this book. Compared with many other disciplines computer programming is, in many respects, still in its infancy, and continues to evolve at a rapid pace. So what do we do next? The next few paragraphs will recap what we've covered and also provide some recommendations for next steps.

Programming Fundamentals
One of the goals for this book was to provide the reader with a solid foundation in computer programming. With that in mind the book includes chapters that focus on fundamentals like the elements of a computer program, the structure of programming languages, the different styles of programs, how programs are executed by a computer, and general computer hardware basics. You also learned the importance of computer program security and experimented with tools that can help you become more efficient and productive at programming.

A great tool for mastering the basics of computer programming is the Alice educational software package (http://www.alice.org). Alice is a 3D programming environment that teaches fundamental programming concepts in the context of creating animations and simple video games. It provides a graphical, drag and drop interface that enables you to create programs by manipulating objects (e.g. people, animals, and vehicles). Alice is free software that is available for the Windows, Mac, and Linux platforms, so I recommend that you check it out.

Languages

While reading this book you learned the basics of several programming languages, and reviewed (or perhaps even programmed) one or more of the provided examples. There are many programming languages currently in use, and they are used to write programs that serve many purposes: general-purpose computing, specialized functions in various domains, entertainment, education, etc. Once the basic programming concepts are well understood I recommend that you become proficient in one programming language and then add others as your needs/interests evolve. You can pick the first language by deciding what area of programming interests you most and then picking a supported language(s). For example, if you would like to start off with web programming, then learning more about HTML, CSS, and JavaScript is a great next step. I recommend starting off by developing a good understanding of HTML, as it is the foundation of web programming. HTML 5 is the latest version of the standard; although it is not fully complete yet, many of its features are supported on the major browsers. Next tackle CSS to learn how to present your content on web pages. Finally you can dive into JavaScript to create the dynamic, feature-rich web pages you're used to seeing.

If you plan on doing general-purpose computing or trying your hand at something like mobile apps or game development, then you may want to take a look at a language that supports this type of programming. In this case, key concerns will be the tool support and software libraries provided along with the computing platform you decide to use – for example if you use Windows, then Visual Basic or Visual C# are good programming language choices for getting started, whereas on the Mac platform Objective-C is a great choice. The Java programming language is supported on multiple platforms.

If, on the other hand, you would like to learn more about higher-level programming models, then you may want to take a look at a functional or logic programming language. As a matter of fact, logic programming is the subject of Appendix A, so stay tuned!

Software Categories

Early in this book we identified the different categories of software (system, application, programming tools). The book also includes chapters on several common types of application software – specifically web programming, social networking, mobile apps, computer graphics, and game programming. There are many categories of software and we've just looked at a few of the more popular ones. Depending upon your interest, you may want to look into other areas like educational software, enterprise software, information software, etc. There are many types of software developed today at various levels of complexity, so you have plenty of options at your disposal to continue your computer programming.

Where to Find Help

If you are having problems understanding a concept or having trouble developing a program, there are plenty of resources you can turn to for help. The **Glossary** provides a short definition of key terms used in this book and the **Resources** appendix includes references to useful documentation and online resources. Each of the technologies we have learned about have active online communities that are great resources to learn more and get help on a topic, here are links to a few.

- **Alice Forum**
  http://www.alice.org/community/
- **Programming Forums**
  http://www.programmingforums.org/
- **W3Schools Forums (HTML, CSS, JavaScript, etc.)**
  http://w3schools.invisionzone.com/
- **iOS Developer Forum**
  http://www.iphonedevsdk.com/
- **Visual Basic .NET Forum**
  http://www.vbdotnetforums.com/forum.php
- **Facebook Developers Forum**
  http://forum.developers.facebook.net/
- **Processing Forum**
  http://forum.processing.org/
- **Kobold2D Forum**
  http://cocos2d-central.com/forum/50-kobold2d-for-ios-mac-os-x/
- **Prolog Forum**
  http://www.tek-tips.com/threadminder.cfm?pid=345

Finally, if you have any questions related to this book, feel free to check out the **Programming for Everyone** website (http://www.motupresse.com/p4e). It contains plenty of example code, recommendations, and additional resources that will be of help as you continue to learn more programming.

Appendix A: Prolog

Prolog is a general-purpose, declarative, *logic programming* language. It was one of the first logic languages developed. There are many implementations of Prolog available today so it is very easy to get started using the language. Now you may be wondering, "Why another programming language, haven't we already looked at enough of them?" Well, it is true that we have learned about several programming languages so far and even written programs with some of them, but you have yet to encounter a logic programming language. Logic programming requires a different approach to programming from what you've learned so far, so this is a good time to learn about it. With that in mind, this section provides an overview of logic programming, compares it to some of the other types of programming styles that you've learned about, and then shows you how to apply this knowledge by writing your first programs using Prolog.

Logic Programming

Logic programming is a type of declarative programming, so let's begin with an overview of this programming style. Earlier in this book we stated that declarative programming focuses on describing what a program should do rather than how it should do it. In addition, programming languages that support this style are *referentially transparent*, meaning its programming expressions always produce the same result for a given set of inputs and don't modify external program state. Logic programming extends this foundation with mathematical logic, implemented using *queries* and *relations*.

OK, I know that some of you may be thinking, "mathematical logic, now what am I getting myself into!" Trust me, as you read this chapter you'll see that this isn't so bad. When you develop a program using the logic programming approach you express an algorithm, a computation, etc. (in essence, its *logic*) in terms of fundamental relations (represented as *facts* and *rules*), and one or more propositions or *goals*. Next you load the program and ask questions (i.e. *queries*) using the language's interpreter. The interpreter then attempts to find the collection of fundamental relations that prove the goal(s) and thus provide answers to the questions, i.e. solutions. So, you could say that logic programming uses the process of theorem proving to execute code! This programming style differs from imperative programming languages we have studied earlier (such as Java or Objective-C) where you write programs that implement a solution by specifying a sequence of instructions. The difference between the imperative and logic programming approaches is somewhat like the difference between computation and deduction. With imperative programming you are **computing** a result based on a specific set of instructions that implement a solution. With logic programming you **deduce** a result based on relations that implement solutions. Another way to think about logic programming is like this: you write a program that describes the *world* (in terms of goals, facts and rules), load this program into the computer, and then ask questions about this world (using queries) to obtain the answers.

Some key concepts that you need to understand to write programs using the logic programming style are relations, logical inference, proof search, backtracking, and resolution. So, before we go any further, let's take a little time to understand what these mean.

Relations
As you can see from the previous section, relations are central to logic programming. A relation describes a connection between one or more things, also called *elements*; it is notated as follows

```
name(element1, element2, ...)
```

Where `name` is the name of the relation and the elements of the relation are in parentheses, separated by commas. For instance, the relation

```
automobile(ferrari)
```

Maps "ferrari" to "automobile", in other words a Ferrari is a type of automobile. A relation could also have multiple elements; these elements may describe elements of the relation, e.g.

```
square(5, 25)
```

The above relation asserts that the square of the number 5 (in other words the product of 5 * 5) equals 25. A relation can be either a fact or a rule – facts are by definition true, a rule is evaluated to prove it is true. Relations are used to prove a theorem through the process of deduction or *logical inference*.

Logical Inference

Logic programming employs theorems, or *logical propositions* involving one or more fundamental relations. The truth of a logical proposition is inferred based on the truth of its relations; this is what is meant by theorem proving. The evaluation of these relations is the mechanism for implementing program code. A logical proposition might look something like the following

```
automobile(m3) ← automobile(bmw), bmw(m3)
```

This proposition asserts that an M3 is an automobile. To prove it is true, the relations `automobile(bmw)` and `bmw(m3)` must be proved true. Relations may include code that implements algorithms, performs computations, etc. A logic program interpreter evaluates these relations (thereby executing the associated code) by *proof search*.

Proof Search

Proof search, or the process of evaluating relations to find a set that proves a proposition, can be performed using several different strategies. The *goal-directed* strategy searches backwards from the initial proposition, while the *forward-reasoning* strategy work forwards from the fundamental relations.

In most logic languages, and Prolog in particular, goal-directed proof search is performed using *Horn clauses*. A Horn clause is a logical proposition that consists of a *head* term (**H**), and one or more relations, known as body terms (**B**). It is written as follows

$$H \leftarrow B_1, B_2, B_3, \ldots$$

What this expression means is that if all the **B** terms evaluate to `true`, we can infer that the proposition **H** is `true` as well (and you have executed the associated code). As an example, for the proposition

```
automobile(m3) ← automobile(bmw), bmw(m3)
```

With the head term

H – m3 is an automobile

And body terms

B₁ - bmw is an automobile
B₂ – m3 is a bmw

We can deduce that the proposition **H** is `true` if the body terms **B₁** and **B₂** evaluate to `true`.

Resolution and Unification

Now that you understand proof search and Horn clauses, you may be wondering, how is this used to prove a proposition consisting of multiple relations? Specifically what is the process by which logic programming systems move from one relation to another, if necessary deriving new relations in the process? Logic programming systems do this using a single inference rule that combines existing statements, canceling like terms, through a process known as *resolution*. The terms can be constants or variables. For instance, if we know that **A** and **B** imply **C** and that **C** implies **D**, we can deduce that **A** and **B** imply **D**. A corresponding example would be

*If a **beagle** is a **dog***
*And **dogs** are **mammals***
*Then a **beagle** is a **mammal**.*

Logic programming systems also compute values for variables through substitution of the values or expressions in matching terms; this process is known as *unification*. Taking the following example

```
mammal(X) ← dog(X)
dog(beagle)
```

The logic program interpreter will assign the value `beagle` to the variable X as it is the only value that can be substituted into the clauses so that they both evaluate to true. Unification enables logic programming systems to bind values or expressions to matching terms.

Backtracking

The body terms of a Horn clause specify the rules used to prove a proposition/theorem. A Horn clause can more than one set of body terms, as there are potentially multiple ways to prove a theorem. If this is the case then a proof search may have multiple paths that can be explored. For example a proposition **H** may have the following two sets of terms.

$$H \leftarrow B_1, B_2, B_3, B_4$$
$$H \leftarrow B_1, B_2, B_5, B_6$$

The point after B_2 at which terms B_3, B_4 or B_5, B_6 can be evaluated is called a *choice point*. If the first attempt at a proof fails, then a logic programming system will try each available alternate path until the proof succeeds or all paths are exhausted; this process is called *backtracking*. With the above example, if B_1 and B_2 evaluate to true, then the B_3, B_4 path is evaluated. If either B_3 or B_4 evaluates to false, then the second path after B_1, B_2 (i.e. B_5, B_6) is tried. You can think of backtracking as a means of "retracing your steps" when attempting to find a solution to a problem. If you think about it for a moment you probably use this kind of approach yourself when you are doing puzzles (crosswords, sudoku, etc.) or solving other sorts of problems. Backtracking is a powerful technique for efficiently solving problems with constraints that have a number of potential solutions.

These are some of the key elements of logic programming. Now that you have a basic understanding of them, hold on tight, because you're about to learn how to write programs with Prolog!

Using Prolog

Prolog stands for **Pro**gramming in **Log**ic. It was developed in the early 1970s and initially associated with natural language processing. It has been widely used for artificial intelligence and is also used in other areas such as expert systems, games, theorem proving, and control systems.

A Prolog interpreter runs within the context of a database of relations consisting of Horn clauses; each clause is comprised of facts and rules (that contain your program code). Using the interpreter you run queries against these clauses to have them evaluated and hence perform computations.

Basic Terms

Each clause is made up of terms of which there are four kinds: *atoms, numbers, variables,* and *compound terms.* Atoms and numbers can also be grouped together as *atomic terms.*

An **atom** is usually a text string made up of letters, digits, and/or an underscore, starting with a lowercase letter. For example, the following are valid atoms:

```
dog, cat, theWord, k123, this_is_a_Prolog_atom
```

An atom can also be a series of characters enclosed in single quotes such as

```
'This is also a Prolog atom.'
```

Strings made up solely of special Prolog characters (e.g., + - * = < > : &) are also atoms.

A **number** is an integer, written as a sequence of digits with a corresponding minus sign (-) if the number is negative.

A **variable** is a string of letters, digits, and/or an underscore, starting with a capital letter or an underscore. For example, the following are valid variables:

```
Monkey, _var123, MyVariable, A_simple_var_
```

The underscore character by itself is also a variable; it is called the *anonymous* variable.

A **compound term** consists of an atom and a number of *arguments* (i.e. atoms, numbers, variables, or other compound terms) enclosed in parentheses and separated by commas. There is no space between the atom and the opening parenthesis. The following are valid compound terms.

```
greeting(name, salutation)
factorial(7)
```

A term that doesn't contain any variables is called a *ground term.* There are several special types of compound terms: predicates, lists, and strings. A *list* is an ordered collection of terms surrounded by square brackets with each term separated by commas. A *string* is a sequence of characters surround by quotes.

Predicates

Prolog supports the notion of a **predicate**. A predicate is named with a compound term, and hence may have one or more arguments. A predicate is defined by a collection of clauses and its value is either true or false; for example if `mammal` is the name of a predicate, then `mammal(dog)` is `true` and `mammal(spider)` is `false`. Typically you implement your program code with predicates; as predicates can have arguments this facilitates the data input values and variables for assigning the output of computations. All Prolog implementations include a number of built-in predicates that provide functionality similar to the software libraries of other programming languages.

Facts and Rules

A **fact** is written as a predicate followed by a dot. It defines a certain instance of a relation as being true, for example

```
mammal(dog).
fish(shark).
```

A **rule** consists of a *head* predicate and a *body*, separated by the sign `:-` and terminated by a dot. A rule body is a sequence of predicates separated by commas. The meaning of a rule is that the head predicate is true if the body (i.e., all the predicates of the body) is true. The above two facts are the same as the rules

```
mammal(dog)  :- true.
fish(shark)  :- true.
```

The sign :- means *implies*, in other words the above rule implies that `mammal(dog)` is true. Multiple body terms in a rule are separated by a comma that indicates "and". For example the rule

```
is_mammal(X)  :- dog(X), mammal(dog).
```

Implies that "for all X, if X is a dog and dogs are mammals, then X is a mammal". Given the above facts and rules if you ask the question (i.e. submit the following queries)

```
?- mammal(dog).
?- fish(shark).
```

The Prolog interpreter will return an answer of `Yes`/`true`. If you state a fact (via the `assert` predicate and then ask a question pertaining to the corresponding rule

```
?- assert(dog(beagle)).
?- is_mammal(beagle).
```

The Prolog interpreter will return `Yes`/`true`.

Lists provide the capability for managing collections of data elements. A list is surrounded by square brackets with its elements separated by commas, for example

```
[elephant, horse, donkey, dog]
```

The list elements can be any valid Prolog terms, i.e. atoms, numbers, variables, compound terms, or even other lists. An empty list is written with just square brackets, i.e. `[]`.

Program One - Factorials

Let's say that you need to implement a program that will compute the factorial of a number. You may remember from your studies of mathematics that a factorial of a positive integer *n*, also written as *n!*, is the product of all positive integers less than or equal to *n*. For example

5! = 5 x 4 x 3 x 2 x 1 = 120

A function/subroutine written to compute a factorial using an imperative programming language (such as ANSI-C) is shown below.

```
int factorial (unsigned int num)
{
  if (num == 0)
  {
    return 1;
  }
  int result = 1;
  for (int ii=1; ii<=num; ++ii)
  {
    result *= ii;
  }
  return result;
}
```

Notice how this program specifies the exact sequence of steps to compute the solution; in this case we used a loop to multiply each number in the factorial sequence. The same program written using Prolog is shown here.

```
/* Factorial program - facts */
factorial(0, 1).          % 0! = 1 (base case)


/* Factorial program - rules */
/* Use recursion, assign result to Val */
factorial(N, Val) :-    % (recursive step)
  N > 0,                 % If N > 0
    M is N - 1,          % Then set M = N-1
    factorial(M, Temp),  % Temp = (N-1)!
    Val is Temp * N.% Val = N * (N-1)!
/* Compute factorial and display the result */
factorial(N) :-
  factorial(N, Product),
    write(Product).
```

Although this program performs the same function as the one written above using ANSI-C, its structure is very different. It is composed of *facts* and *rules* that completely describe it; the facts state information about the world (or in this case the algorithm) that you are describing, and the rules define relations. Notice also that this program uses *recursion;* we'll discuss this shortly. After you write and save a Prolog program you compile it; this loads the program's relations (i.e. its facts and rules) into the Prolog interpreter's database. Now you can submit a query to the interpreter based on these relations (for example, ask for the factorial of a given number); in response the interpreter executes the query (by evaluating its associated relations) and, if it (proof search) succeeds, it returns the corresponding results. Using the factorial program the following query

```
?- factorial(5).
120
true
```

was successfully evaluated, hence the Prolog interpreter returned both the result of the evaluation (i.e. the correct printed value of 120) and true (to indicate that the relation was proved, i.e. proof search succeeded).

Recursion

Recursion, at its base, refers to something reoccurring or repeating. In the field of computer science, recursion is an approach to solving problems whereby you take the original problem and divide it into smaller (and more easily solved) instances of itself, solve those, and then assemble the results into the final solution. Many mathematical theorems are based on recursive rules. Programming languages usually support this technique by enabling functions to call themselves. Likewise a Prolog predicate can call itself. The factorial algorithm can be defined with recursion (i.e., **n! = (n – 1)! * n**); and this is implemented in the Prolog factorial program shown above.

Program Two – Fibonacci Sequence

Now we're going to create a program that retrieves a number from the Fibonacci sequence. Fibonacci numbers follow the sequence

0, 1, 1, 2, 3, 5, 8, 13, 21, 34, 55, 89, ...

By definition, the first two numbers in the Fibonacci sequence are 0 and 1, and each subsequent number is the sum of the previous two. In mathematical terms, a number in the Fibonacci sequence is defined by the recursive relation

$$F_n = F_{n-1} + F_{n-2}$$

where the first two values are

$$F_0 = 0 \text{ and } F_1 = 1$$

So, if the user requests the third number in the sequence the program should return 1; for the fourth number it should return 2; for the fifth number it returns 3; the sixth it should return 5; and so on.

We'll develop this program step-by-step; first we'll download and install a Prolog implementation. Next we'll start the Prolog system and develop the Fibonacci program. Finally we'll compile the program and use the Prolog interpreter to test the program by submitting some queries to return numbers in the Fibonacci sequence.

Install SWI-Prolog (Step 1)

There are numerous Prolog implementations available; for this example we are going to use **SWI-Prolog**, a free, widely used Prolog environment that runs on Mac, Windows, and Linux systems. You can download SWI-Prolog from the SWI Prolog home page (http://www.swi-prolog.org). Download the appropriate version for your system and install it per the instructions provided at the website.

Develop Fibonacci Program (Step 2)

Now we'll develop the Fibonacci program. Depending upon the system you are using (Mac/Windows/Linux), startup the SWI-Prolog program as follows:

- **Windows**
  Double-clicking **swipl-win.exe** file in the location where you installed it.
- **Mac/Linux**
  The SWI-Prolog application is by default installed in the /opt/local/bin directory. A startup shortcut is currently not provided, hence to start the program open up a terminal window (you Mac and Linux people know what these are!) and type **/opt/local/bin/swipl** followed by a carriage return.

Note that the Windows SWI-Prolog program provides some additional features; in particular it includes an interactive environment within which you can create, run, and debug programs. For this example we'll use the Windows SWI-Prolog version (instructions will also be provided for users of the Mac/Linux version). Once started the Prolog environment will display a window with a menu of options.

Figure 79. SWI-Prolog Main Window

Next we'll create a new file for the program. On Windows systems you can create a file from the File menu; select the **File → New...** option. A window will be displayed, titled **Create new Prolog source**. In the **File name:** text field at the bottom of the window, type the word **factorial** and click the **Save** button; this will create and save the **factorial.pl** program file.

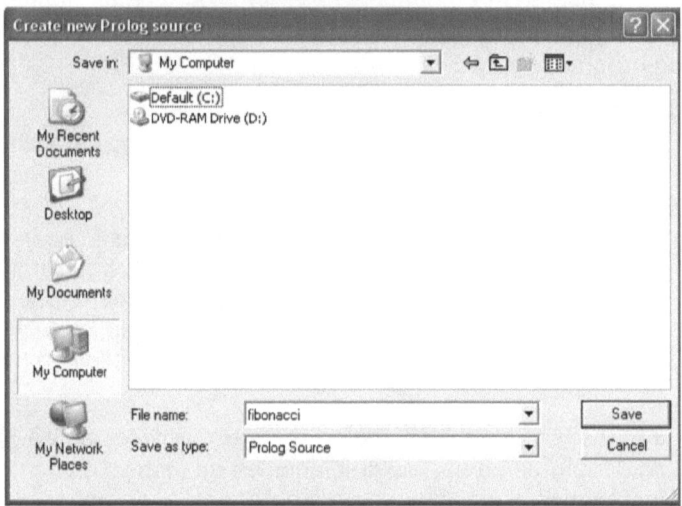

Figure 80. Create new Prolog source Window

After clicking the above-mentioned Save button, a new window (the SWI-Prolog Editor) is displayed that allows you to edit, compile, and debug your program. From this window we will write our program.

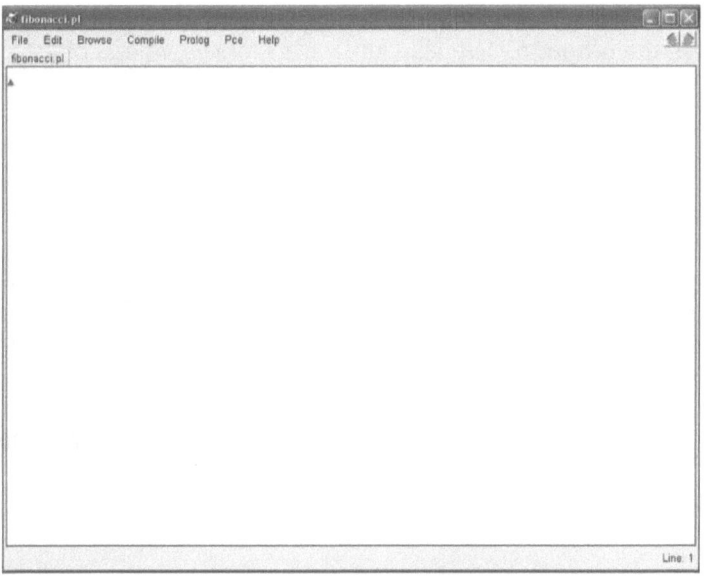

Figure 81. SWI-Prolog Editor Window

On Mac/Linux systems, you should create a new file named **factorial.pl** *in the same directory from which you started the SWI-Prolog program. As the Mac/Linux version has no text editor, you'll then edit the file using your text editor of choice (on Mac systems this would most typically be **TextEdit**).*

We can now use the SWI-Prolog Editor to edit, compile, and debug the fibonacci.pl file. In addition to commands for the above functions, the Editor also includes a command to save the file currently being edited (**File ➜ Save buffer**); you should save your work often!

OK, now it's time to implement the Fibonacci sequence. We know that a recursive relation defines it, so all we have to do is implement this in Prolog. When implementing a recursive relation, we need to have implement code to stop the algorithm from calling itself indefinitely (i.e. the *base case*) and code for the actual recursive algorithm. For example, in order to compute the 5th number (F_5) in the Fibonacci sequence we have to compute all the numbers before it as specified in the recursive relation.

$$F_n = F_{n-1} + F_{n-2}$$

This relation corresponds to a Prolog rule, so we will implement that in the program. We also know the first two values of the sequence.

$F_0 = 0$

$F_1 = 1$

These correspond to facts in Prolog, so we'll implement these in the program as well. Let's start by implementing the facts first; in Prolog a **fact** relation is implemented with a compound term that consists of a name followed by a number of variables in parentheses that specify the corresponding relation. Let's name our relation `fibonacci`. The relation we have is between Fibonacci sequence elements and the value for each of these elements. The first fact asserts that the value of the 0th number in the Fibonacci sequence is 0. Likewise the second fact asserts that value for the 1st number in the sequence is 1. Using the Editor add the following lines of code.

```
fibonacci(0,0).
fibonacci(1,1).
```

This code implements the two facts for the relation named `fibonacci`. Now that we have implemented the base cases we will implement the recursive algorithm. The recursive relation is implemented as a rule in Prolog, so we must write this code. Recall from earlier that a rule consists of a head predicate and one or more body terms. Let's start by writing the code for the head proposition; add the following line of code below the facts

```
fibonacci(N,Value) :-
```

This code is the head proposition; but this time the relation has variable arguments **N** and **Value**. When implemented this relation can be used to compute the **Value** of an arbitrary N^{th} element in the Fibonacci sequence – we already have the relation for the base cases. We now need to add the correct body terms that evaluate to `true`, thereby proving the proposition (and hence performing the computation). We know the algorithm states that the value of a Fibonacci number equals the sum of the two proceeding numbers, so how do we get those numbers? This is where recursion is employed; we can use this technique to recursively retrieve the two proceeding numbers. We do this until we count down to the base case, then one-by-one compute the value for each number in the sequence up to the desired value in the sequence. For example, to get the value of the 4th element in the Fibonacci sequence, we need to get the

3rd element in the sequence
2nd element in the sequence
1st element in the sequence

Now we know the values of both the 1st element in the sequence (1) and the 0th element (0) – remember these were coded above as facts, so we use this to compute the value of the 2nd element as the sum of the previous two (1 + 0 = 1). Next we can compute the value of the 3rd element as 1 + 1 = 2. Finally we compute the value of the 4th element as 2 + 1 = 3. What this means is that each time we invoke the fibonacci rule for any particular number in the sequence, we will recursively invoke the rule on the previous two numbers in the sequence. This will continue until we count down to the 1st element in the sequence. Now update the fibonacci rule using the Editor as follows.

```
fibonacci(0,0).
fibonacci(1,1).

fibonacci(N,Value) :-
  N > 1,
  N1 is N - 1,
  N2 is N - 2,
  fibonacci(N1,Tmp1),
  fibonacci(N2,Tmp2),
  Value is Tmp1 + Tmp2.
```

We added body terms to completely implement the rule as described above. Let's review each term, starting with the first one

```
  N > 1,
```

If this term evaluates to true (in other words the element in the sequence is greater than 1) the interpreter will continue evaluating the other body terms. Hence this stops the recursion once we have counted down to the 1st element in the sequence. The next two terms

```
  N1 is N - 1,
  N2 is N - 2,
```

Retrieve the numbers of the two previous elements. The next two terms

```
fibonacci(N1,Tmp1),
fibonacci(N2,Tmp2),
```

Recursively evaluate the Fibonacci relation, using the previous two numbers retrieved above. The values for these numbers are stored in temporary variables. The last term

```
Value is Tmp1 + Tmp2.
```

sums the values for the two previous values in the sequence. The program is again shown below, this time with comments

```
/* Fibonacci sequence - facts */
fibonacci(0,0).            % F_0 = 0
fibonacci(1,1).            % F_1 = 1

/* Fibonacci sequence - rules */
fibonacci(N,Value) :-
  N > 1,                   % For numbers above 1
  N1 is N - 1,             % Use previous
  N2 is N - 2,             % 2 numbers
  fibonacci(N1,Tmp1),      % Get values for these
  fibonacci(N2,Tmp2),
  Value is Tmp1 + Tmp2. % And add per relation
```

And that's it; we have implemented the complete program. In the Editor save the program (**File ➔ Save buffer**) and then compile it (**Compile ➔ Compile buffer**). After compiling look at the output from the SWI-Prolog Main Window; you should see the following

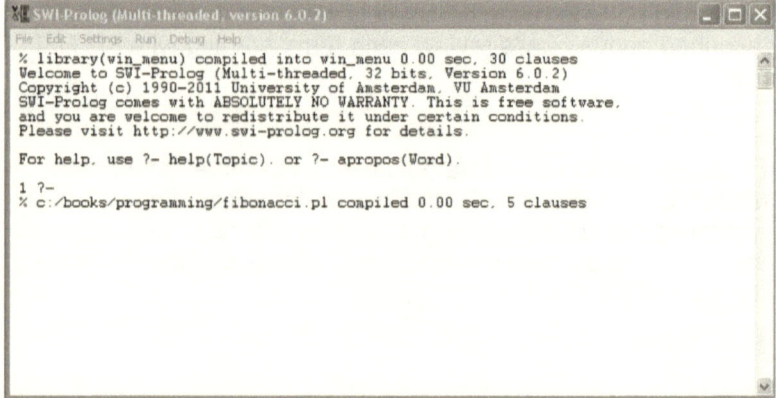

Figure 82. Compilation Results

On Mac/Linux systems, you load and compile the program by specifying the file name (its full path, without the .pl extension) between brackets and quotes. For example, if the file was created in directory /Users/prolog *then from the Mac/Linux SWI-Prolog window you should type the command below followed by a carriage return.*

```
?- ['Users/prolog/fibonacci'].
```

Now we can test the program by submitting some queries in the Main window and verifying that the program computes the expected results. First type a period to terminate the compilation results, and then try the following queries.

```
?- fibonacci(3, X).
```

```
?- fibonacci(4, X).
```

```
?- fibonacci(7, X).
```

```
?- fibonacci(11, X).
```

```
?- fibonacci(16, X).
```

The results should be as shown below.

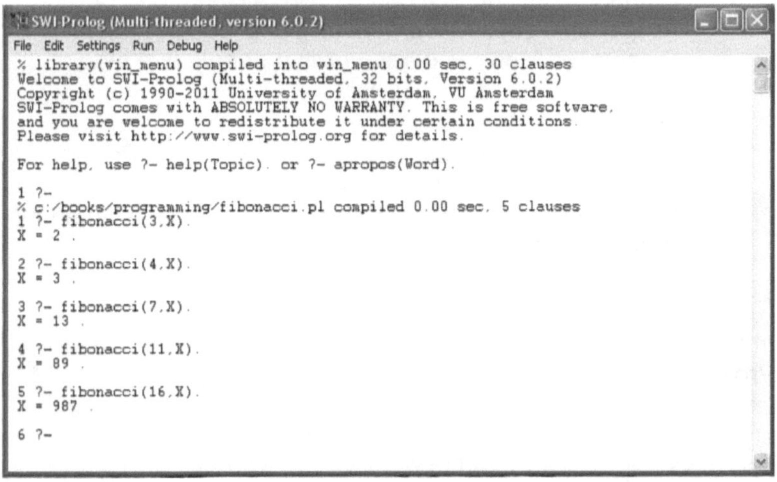

Figure 83. Fibonacci Program Results

If your results differ, carefully review the complete code listing provided above. Make any updates required, then save, compile, and run the program again using the listed inputs. Now congratulations are definitely in order; you have implemented your first program using Prolog!

Prolog Key Features

Some of the key features of Prolog are:

- Logic programming paradigm
  Logic programming is a type of declarative programming that incorporates mathematical logic for performing computations. Prolog is the most popular logic programming language.
- Values, variables, and terms
  Each Prolog clause is made up of values, variables, and/or terms. These are the basic terms (i.e. statements and expressions) of a Prolog program.
- Assertions and clauses
  A Prolog assertion defines a relation as being true (i.e. *a dog is a mammal*); a clause (specifically a Horn clause) is comprised of facts and rules that evaluate to true if proved.
- Relations
  A relation describes a connection between one or more things, also called *elements* (e.g dog(beagle) maps "beagle" to "dog", in other words a beagle is a type of dog).
- Queries
  A Prolog query evaluates facts and rules in a Prolog database to determine whether or not it is true (and hence perform a computation). This is accomplished by performing a proof search.

Summary

In this chapter we learned about logic programming and used Prolog, the most popular logic programming language, to implement a few programs. Logic programming is a different style of programming than we used throughout most of this book, and this chapter attempted to provide you with an overview of its main concepts. Declarative programming in general and logic programming in particular are growing in popularity and usage. Having a good understanding of this programming style will be a great asset as you continue on with your computer programming.

Appendix B: Glossary

This glossary consists of definitions for many of the programming terms and concepts discussed in this book.

1st Generation Language
A first-generation programming language is a machine-level language. It directly uses the computer's instruction set and hardware. These were the first languages used to program computers.

2nd Generation Language
A second-generation language is an assembly language that provides basic abstractions from the computer's instruction set and hardware. Typically an assembler is used to convert assembly language programs into machine code that can be executed by the computer.

3rd Generation Language
Third-generation languages feature abstractions that enable more structured programming, facilitate reuse of blocks of code through subroutines, and support numerous data types. Programs written using a 3rd generation language are typically executed using a compiler.

4th Generation Language
Fourth-generation languages have an even greater rich set of control and data abstractions that aim to support high-level specifications, thereby mapping more closely to the problem

domain. Many are designed for building specific types of programs.

5th Generation Language

Fifth-generation languages are designed to enable *constraints-based* programming, whereby a program does not specify the steps involved in performing a computation, but rather defines the constraints associated with the computation and then lets the computer determine the solution. Many constraints-based and logic programming languages are considered 5th generation languages.

Assembly Language

An assembly language is a low-level programming language that provides basic support for abstractions. An assembly language is specific to a computer's hardware architecture.

Class

In object-oriented programming, a class is a specification for an object. It specifies an object's instance variables, properties and methods, and contains the code that implements the programming logic for each method.

Compiler

A compiler is a special type of program that is used to translate a program written in one language (typically a high-level language) into another (typically executable machine code), which means the same thing as the original program. Compilers are typically used to produce machine code that can then be executed by the target computer.

Computer Animation

Computer animation is the process used for generating and displaying a sequence of digital images to create an illusion of movement; it can be performed using techniques such as keyframing, motion capture, and kinematics.

Computer Program

A computer program is a sequence of instructions that perform a specific task (perform a computation, execute an algorithm, etc.) on a computer.

Declarative Programming

Declarative languages describe what something is by identifying its attributes and characteristics, defining its mathematical relations, specifying its rules, etc. Hyper Text Markup Language (HTML) and Extensible Markup Language (XML) are examples of declarative languages. Declarative programming languages focus on defining the logic of a computation (i.e. the desired goal or result) rather than its control flow (i.e. how to perform the computation). Other common characteristics include execution order independence (no side-effects), non-destructive variable assignment, and the use of expressions and definitions as values.

Device Driver
A device driver is a computer program that enables other programs to interact with a hardware device. A driver typically communicates with a device through a communication bus to which it is connected.

Executable
An executable is a file or group of files comprised of program code executed by a computer. An executable may be in the target language of the machine on which the program executes or in an interpreted language.

Expression
An *expression* is a group of one or more numbers and/or symbols that can be evaluated and return a value; an expression is somewhat like a phrase in a natural language.

Function
A *function* is a portion of code within a program that performs a specific task and is relatively independent of the remaining program code.

High-Level Language
A high-level language is a computer programming language that provides numerous abstractions from the details of computers (e.g., the instruction set, hardware specifics, etc.). They are designed to make the process of writing and maintaining programs both simpler and more efficient.

Image Modeling
Three dimensional (3D) image modeling is the process of developing a 3D surface model of any object using software. A 3D model represents a collection of points in 3D space, connected by geometric items such as lines, curved surfaces, triangles, etc. Models can be created automatically or manually, by hand, by algorithm, or scanned.

Image Rendering
Image rendering is the process of generating a two dimensional

(2D) image or animation from a prepared scene. The scene is a description of (view) objects; it contains geometry, viewpoint, texture, and lighting information. Rendering may be 2D or 3D, where 3D rendering converts a 3D model into 2D images. The steps involved in 3D rendering require both determining which parts of a scene to show on the display and how each pixel on the display should look for maximum realism. The most commonly used image rendering techniques are rasterization, ray casting, ray tracing, and radiosity.

Imperative Programming
Imperative programming is a style of computer programming whereby computations are performed through a sequence of commands. In effect, an imperative program specifies, step-by-step, the control flow of a computation (i.e. *how* to obtain the desired results). Characteristically, the order of execution of an imperative program's statements is critical; in addition, program state can be changed as a result of execution.

Interpreter
An interpreter is a special type of program that executes the instructions of a program. It can do this by executing the source code directly or in real-time translating the source code into an intermediate representation and executing that. An interpreter can speed up the development cycle (compared to using a compiler), as source code changes can be immediately tested. However, interpreted programs typically run slower than compiled programs.

JSON
JSON is the abbreviation for JavaScript Object Notation, a standards-based format for textual data. The JSON format supports a number of data types, and is commonly used for exchanging data over the web.

Logic Programming
Logic programming is a type of declarative programming that employs mathematical logic, specifically proof search, for performing computations. In effect, logic programming uses the process of theorem proving to execute code. Prolog is the most popular logic programming language in use today.

Low-Level Language
A low-level language is a programming language that has little support for abstraction from a computer's implementation details. Low-level languages are typically assembly languages; an

assembler is used to convert programs written using assembly language into machine code.

Machine Code
Machine code can be processed by a computer directly without transformation. It is made up of the instructions executed directly by a computer's CPU. Machine code is extremely hardware-dependent and difficult to program.

Markup Language
A markup language is used to annotate a document for some (additional) processing. HTML is the main markup language used structuring web pages and other information that can be displayed in a web browser.

Object-Oriented Programming
Object-Oriented Programming is a style of computer programming for which the chief building blocks of a program (data, instructions for manipulating data) are structured as *software objects*. A software object provides a representation (in software) of the characteristics or attributes of the thing/concept being modeled, along with a definition of the things it can do. An object-oriented program executes its logic by creating object instances and invoking the desired operations on these objects.

Operator
An *operator* is programming language symbol that performs a specific machine instruction; common examples are the addition $(+)$ or subtraction $(-)$ operators.

Programming Abstraction
Programming abstractions are constructs designed to simplify programming by hiding the details of the computer. Programming languages generally support both control and data abstractions.

Software Library
A software library is a collection of resources (code, files, images, etc.) used to develop software. Libraries enable the reuse of code and data that provides common services.

Statement
A programming language *statement* is a complete, standalone language element, somewhat like a sentence in a natural language. It is comprised of symbols, numbers, and/or expressions and is terminated by a symbol or a newline.

Style Sheet Language
A style sheet language is a computer language used to specify the presentation of structured documents. Cascading Style Sheets (CSS) and Extensible Stylesheet Language (XSL) are two of the most commonly used style sheet languages.

Symbol
A programming language *symbol* is somewhat like a word in a natural language – an element of content with practical meaning. In most programming languages symbols are commonly written as a letter followed by zero or more of any characters (excluding whitespace).

Three-Dimensional Graphics
3D computer graphics are mathematical representations of three-dimensional objects that are used to perform calculations and render 2D images. Computer-generated imagery (CGI) is often used to apply 3D computer graphics to special effects in art, video games, films, television programs, commercials, simulations, and printed media.

Two-Dimensional Graphics
2D computer graphics is the computer-based generation of images, primarily from two-dimensional models such as 2D geometric models, text, and digital images, and specific techniques. The most common techniques used to create 2D graphics are raster graphics and vector graphics.

URL
A Uniform Resource Locator (URL) is a string of characters used to identify the path to a resource (web page, image, audio file, etc.) that is accessible over the internet. The general syntax of a URL is

protocol: / / *domain*: *port* / *path*

The *protocol* specifies the communications protocol for the URL (i.e. http, https, ftp, etc.) The *domain* specifies the domain name or IP address for the destination resource, in other words its website address. The *port* is an optional decimal value that indicates the port used for the website; if not provided the default port for the protocol is used. For example the default port for http-based communication is 80. The *path* specifies the resource requested; it may include details on how to find the resource and/or information to be passed to the server that hosts the website.

XML

The Extensible Markup Language (XML) is a markup language that defines a set of rules for describing data. XML is generally used to define data elements on web pages and electronic documents. It is the most common format used for electronic data interchange.

Appendix C: Resources

There is a wealth of documentation available (both online and in print) for learning more about programming. There are also numerous mailing lists, discussion forums, blogs, and web sites that you can seek out for helpful advice. The next few pages are a sampling of the many resources and documentation available on the topics covered in this book.

Object-Oriented Programming
Object-Oriented Programming Concepts, Exforsys Inc, http://www.exforsys.com/tutorials/oops.html.

Object-Oriented Programming Tutorial, Aonaware, http://www.aonaware.com/OOP1.htm.

Object Oriented Programming, Wikibooks, http://en.wikibooks.org/wiki/Object_Oriented_Programming.

Objective-C
Core Objective-C in 24 Hours, Keith Lee, Motu Presse Publications, http://www.motupresse.com.

The Objective-C Programming Language, Apple Developer Library, https://developer.apple.com/.

Learning Objective-C: A Primer, Apple Developer Library, https://developer.apple.com/.

Object-Oriented Programming with Objective-C, Apple Developer Library, https://developer.apple.com/.

Apple Developer, https://developer.apple.com/.

Web Programming
HTML Tutorial, W3 Schools,
http://www.w3schools.com/html/default.asp.

CSS Tutorial, W3 Schools,
http://www.w3schools.com/css/default.asp.

Javascript Tutorial, W3 Schools,
http://www.w3schools.com/js/default.asp.

HTML, XHTML, and CSS, E. Castro, Cookwood Press.

Mobile App Development
Live Code Mobile Development Beginner's Guide, C. Holgate,
Packt Press.

iOS Dev Center, Apple Developer,
https://developer.apple.com/iphone.

iPhone and iPad Apps for Absolute Beginners, R. Lewis, Apress
Publications.

Android Developers, http://www.android.com.

Android Apps for Absolute Beginners, W. Jackson, Apress
Publications.

Secure Coding
Introduction to Secure Coding Guide,
https://developer.apple.com/library/mac/documentation/security/c
onceptual/SecureCodingGuide/SecureCodingGuide.pdf.

Secure Coding Guidelines for the Java Programming Language,
http://www.oracle.com/technetwork/java/seccodeguide-
139067.html.

OWASP Secure Coding Principles,
https://www.owasp.org/index.php/Secure_Coding_Principles.

Microsoft Secure Coding Guidelines,
http://msdn.microsoft.com/en-us/library/8a3x2b7f.aspx.

Computer Graphics
Processing website, http://processing.org.

Generative Art, M. Pearson, Manning Publications.

Getting Started with Processing, C. Reas & B. Fry, O'Reilly &
Associates.

Introduction to Computer Graphics Using Java 2D and 3D, F. Klawonn, Springer.

Computer Graphics Programs, W3 Professors, http://www.w3professors.com/Pages/Courses/Computer-Graphics/Programs/CG-Program.html.

Interactive Computer Graphics, A Top-Down Approach Using Open GL, 5/E, E. Angel, Addison-Wesley.

Game Programming
GameDev Developer Community, http://www.gamedev.net/page/index.html.

Kobold2D website, http://www.kobold2d.com.

Cocos2d for iPhone website, http://www.cocos2d-iphone.org/.

Learn cocos2D Game Development with iOS 5, S. Itterheim, A. Low, Apress Publications.

Visual Basic Game Programming Tutorial for Beginners, http://computersight.com/programming/visual-basic-game-programming-tutorial-for-beginners/.

Unity 3D Game Development by Example Beginner's Guide, R. Creighton, Packt Publications.

Logic Programming
Programming in Prolog, W. Clocksin and C. Mellish, Springer.

Prolog, Wikibooks, http://en.wikibooks.org/wiki/Prolog.

Learn Prolog Now!, http://www.learnprolognow.org/.

SWI-Prolog website, http://www.swi-prolog.org/.

Index

anteof

www.ingramcontent.com/pod-product-compliance
Lightning Source LLC
Chambersburg PA
CBHW030004190526
45157CB00014B/426